6/09

BUSTED

Busted

LIFE INSIDE THE GREAT MORTGAGE MELTDOWN

Edmund L. Andrews

W. W. Norton & Company   New York London

For information about permission to reproduce selections from this book,
write to Permissions, W. W. Norton & Company, Inc.,
500 Fifth Avenue, New York, NY 10110

For information about special discounts for bulk purchases, please contact
W. W. Norton Special Sales at specialsales@wwnorton.com or 800-233-4830

Manufacturing by RR Donnelley, Harrisonburg
Production manager: Julia Druskin

Library of Congress Cataloging-in-Publication Data

Andrews, Edmund L.
Busted : life inside the great mortgage meltdown / Edmund L. Andrews.
p. cm.
ISBN 978-0-393-06794-1 (hardcover)
1. Mortgages—United States. 2. Subprime mortgage loans—United States.
3. Housing—United States—Finance. 4. Housing—Prices—United States.
I. Title.
HG2040.5.U5A753 2009
332.7'20973—dc22
2009009074

W. W. Norton & Company, Inc.
500 Fifth Avenue, New York, N.Y. 10110
www.wwnorton.com

W. W. Norton & Company Ltd.
Castle House, 75/76 Wells Street, London W1T 3QT

1 2 3 4 5 6 7 8 9 0

To Patty, for richer or poorer.
To the lights of our lives—Emily, Will, Matthew,
Daniel, Ryan, Sam, and Ben.
And to The House, which left me wiser if poorer.

Contents

Contents

Introduction

If there is anybody who should have avoided the mortgage catastrophe, it is me. As an economics reporter for *The New York Times,* I have been the paper's chief eyes and ears on the Federal Reserve for the past six years. I watched Alan Greenspan and his successor, Ben S. Bernanke, at close range. I wrote several early-warning stories in 2004 about the spike in go-go mortgages. Before that, I had a hand in covering the Asian financial crisis of 1997, the Russia meltdown in 1998, and the dot-com collapse in 2000. I had learned a lot about the curveballs that the economy can throw at us.

But in 2004, I joined millions of otherwise sane Americans in what we now know was a catastrophic binge on overpriced real estate and reckless mortgages. As I write in February 2009, I am four months past due on my mortgage and bracing for foreclosure proceedings to begin.

Nobody duped me, hypnotized me, or lulled me with drugs. Like so many others—borrowers, lenders, and the Wall Street deal makers behind them—I thought I could beat the odds. Everybody had a reason for getting in trouble. The brokers and deal makers were scoring huge commissions. The condo flippers were aiming for quick profits. The ordinary home buyers wanted to own their first houses, or bigger houses, or vacation houses. Some were greedy, some were desperate, and some were deceived. Maybe some were like me: in love.

Whatever our individual stories, the consequences of this nationwide bender are apparent. Wall Street's most iconic firms have been decimated, and the commercial banking system is effectively bankrupt. Bear Stearns and Lehman Brothers are gone. Merrill Lynch is the ravaged subsidiary of Bank of America, which itself is on life support from the federal government. Citigroup is a zombie bank. American International Group, once the nation's largest insurance company, is now an extremely expensive ward of the state.

Beyond the institutional wreckage, Americans are poorer than they were a few years ago. By the end of 2008, one out of eleven home mortgages was either delinquent or in foreclosure, according to the Mortgage Bankers Association. One out of every six homes was underwater, meaning that the mortgage amount was higher than the market value of the house. The number of families that had lost their homes to foreclosure had more than doubled since the housing bubble peaked, from just over 900,000 in 2006 to a new record of 2.2 million in 2008. As I write, analysts are predicting that at least 3 million homes will enter foreclosure in 2009 unless the government rescues them.

Between collapsing home prices and collapsing stock prices, the

United States has lost about $12 trillion in wealth over the past two years. It is tempting to dismiss that figure as "paper losses," but it amounts to a gigantic hole in the nation's balance sheet that will take years to repair. Meanwhile, the United States has almost single-handedly tipped the rest of the global economy into its worst downturn in decades.

This book describes in gory detail how I got it wrong and the personal nightmare that followed, but its broader purpose is to explore how so many other people also went wrong. I know why I borrowed nearly a half-million dollars. The mystery is why so many people were so eager to lend it to me—not once, but three times.

What were we thinking? How hard was it to understand the risks we were taking? Didn't we learn anything from the speculative bubble and bust of dot-com stocks in 2000?

I decided to explore that question by learning about the people who helped deliver the money to my door—the mortgage brokers and real estate appraisers, the lenders and the Wall Street securitizers, the credit rating agencies who blessed the deals, and the institutional investors who paid top dollar for a piece of the action.

I became an expert on the exotic new tools of home finance: a rainbow of "no-doc" and "low-doc" loans; interest-only loans; "piggyback" loans; and "option ARMS," known in various quarters as "pick-a-payment" loans and "exploding ARMS." As I began to drown in debt, I learned that I could borrow even more money and boost my credit rating in the process. Through it all, banks and finance companies happily competed to keep my shell game going.

Misery doesn't love company, but I do take some pride that I outlasted two of my three mortgage lenders. One of them, a high-flier in the subprime business, was shut down by federal regulators in early 2007. Its loans were so bad that it became a catalyst for the panic that kicked off the broader financial crisis in August 2007. Another of my lenders became one of the most immediate victims of that crisis, collapsing overnight in the first week of August and becoming the second biggest bankruptcy of 2007.

The Great American Mortgage Bust wasn't a freak event, like a midsummer snowstorm. It was the result of a trend toward higher debt and greater speculation that had been building for at least twenty-five years. We were taught to borrow more, buy more, save less, and take bigger risks. We learned new financial tricks, grew more confident, and constantly pushed the limits of what seemed acceptable. "Creative financing," an early-1980s phrase that implied shady or stupid deals, was repackaged as "financial innovation." Debt became high-tech, sophisticated, even cool. When the borrowing binge reached its inevitable climax, the fallout engulfed a huge share of the country.

I am not a victim, because I knew full well I was taking a huge gamble. My hunch is that a large share of the people who are now in trouble knew in their gut they were taking unreasonable risks too. Adults who buy homes have to take responsibility for their decisions.

That said, this crisis would not have been possible without breathtaking cynicism on the part of the brainiest people and biggest institutions in American finance. For all the baffling complexities at work—"collateralized debt obligations," "conduits," and computer-run risk models—this is a fairly simple story about how a lot of really smart people embraced and proselytized for a lot of inexcusable hogwash.

"This crisis wasn't an accident. We didn't get unlucky," said David Einhorn, director of Greenlight Capital, a New York City hedge fund, in a speech in October 2007. "This crisis came because there have been a lot of bad practices and bad ideas. . . . Why should anyone be surprised? We got what we deserved." Amen. This was a democratic debacle that made fools out of people up and down the financial food chain. Yet it was worse than that. This was a debacle that stemmed from deep-seated rot and corroded ethics in our financial system.

When I first started digging into this crisis, I was struck by how dumb many of the players seemed. The more I learned, though, the more I became convinced that the blunders were too basic to be written off as boneheaded. Many of the people who should have known better *did* know better. Executives at one of Wall Street's biggest subprime factories, Merrill Lynch, ignored the prescient warnings of their own chief economist about the housing bubble. The rating agencies ignored blatant fallacies in their risk assumptions and compounded the problem by refusing to look at the actual mortgages behind the securities they were rating. Institutional investors went along with the rating agencies, despite a growing chorus of skeptics, because they wanted that extra kick of seemingly free yield that came from triple-A bonds backed by junk loans.

In Washington, of course, the Federal Reserve, the Bush administration, and Congress were ready to believe anything that business told them. When the true character of the crisis became apparent in 2007 and 2008, the Bush administration could not bring itself to believe that something was fundamentally wrong with the financial system or with the dogma of hands-off regulation. As late as December 2007, when the economy was tipping into a recession, President Bush was still confidently declaring that the fundamentals of the economy were sound.

My wife Patty and I may or may not hold on to our house. We most certainly will have to spend years making up the losses from our adventure. But if there is one conclusion I have reached from our experience, it is that our misjudgments, however egregious they were, pale in comparison with the self-enriching recklessness of those at the top of the financial ladder. They were the ones who behaved as if they had invented a perpetual-motion machine. They were the ones who rationalized the "see no evil, hear no evil" model of lending and risk management. For all the money that bankers and Wall Street executives have lost, they are still the ones who walked away from the disaster with tens or hundreds of millions of dollars more than they had at the start. In Washington, the level of malign neglect was every bit as unforgivable.

I have spent my entire adult life a believer in the merits of capitalism, free markets, and the pursuit of enlightened self-interest. I appreciate business and investing, in part because I like the creativity and willingness to take risks that go along with them. I admire entrepreneurs like Steve Jobs and Bill Gates, farsighted investors like Warren Buffett, and shrewd hedge fund managers like John Paulson and David Einhorn. All in all, I am still an economic conservative.

But this catastrophe has reminded us that free markets can become corrupt and self-destructive. Open competition is not always a self-correcting force, and the absence of regulation can be as lethal to capitalism as overregulation. American voters have already drawn the obvious lessons, throwing know-nothing Republicans out of the White House and reducing their ranks in Congress to a shrill but obstreperous minority. President Obama and Democratic lawmakers in Congress may well overshoot in trying to micromanage the economy, and they may well do so at the same time they capitulate to lobbyists from the financial industry. Let's face it: there is no simple balance between free-market dynamism and government oversight.

That is the polite, policy-wonk, *New York Times* side of me talking. On a personal level, I wish I could send one message to the millions of home buyers who made bad choices: don't beat yourself up over your mistakes.

Yes, you might have bought a house you knew in your gut you couldn't afford. Yes, you might have been a fool for not asking tougher questions about your mortgage—or even trying to read the mortgage. Maybe you were a shameless condo flipper who lied about your income on your "no-income-verification" loan, and maybe you've got the bill collectors after you now. From a moral standpoint, you may not deserve any kind of mercy or bailout from the government. I don't honestly think that I do.

Take a cue from the bank or Wall Street firm that is now trying to foreclose on your house. Don't apologize. They knew what they were getting into far better than you did. They knew they were in a giant Ponzi scheme, and they certainly should have known it would lead to disaster. They knew the housing bubble was a mirage. They knew their loans were absurd. They knew the triple-A ratings were bogus. They knew, they knew, they knew. They deserve whatever losses come their way.

BUSTED

1

MONEY FOR NOTHING

Alan Greenspan blanched. First he looked appalled. Then he looked perplexed. And for the first time that I could remember, his patient and gravelly voice turned curt and commanding. "Why did you do it?" he asked, interrupting me in midsentence. I felt like a teenager who had just told his father he had crashed the family car.

There I was, a fifty-two-year-old economics reporter covering the biggest financial calamity since the Great Depression, and I had just blurted out to the former chairman of the Federal Reserve that I was close to defaulting on the same kind of reckless mortgages that were drowning the nation's financial system. "I took a gamble," I answered irritably. "I knew it was a big risk, but I thought that we could manage it."

Going into the meeting, the last thing I had wanted to do was confess that I had succumbed to the same foolish temptations that had trapped millions of other Americans. My credit scores were shot. Bill collectors called constantly. I was flirting with foreclosure. Almost none of our friends or neighbors had any idea how close to the edge my wife Patty and I were. Like countless others trapped in the mortgage meltdown, we looked like average suburban home owners. We grilled hamburgers on the deck, cut the grass on weekends, walked the dog in the mornings, and drove our children to soccer games. We had carefully preserved our image as normal, home-owning neighbors—stable, reliable, and responsible.

In truth, the words *home owner* and *stable* had stopped being inseparable for a lot of people. It was December 2007, and Wall Street had woken to the reality that millions of people who had bought homes with "liar's loans" had—shockingly—lied to get their loans. Delinquency rates and home foreclosure rates were soaring several times higher than the experts and the financial models had ever predicted. In the press, the yuletide buzzword that season was *jingle mail*, house keys mailed back to lenders from people who had walked away from their properties. The trillion-dollar credit markets had been frozen since August, and seemingly immortal institutions like Citigroup and Merrill Lynch were hemorrhaging tens of billions of dollars in mortgage-related losses. Out in the "real economy," tapped-out and stressed-out Americans were starting to buckle.

For two hours, I had been listening to Greenspan explain why he shouldn't be blamed for what was happening. He had just published his best-selling memoir, *The Age of Turbulence,* and he was making as much as $200,000 per speech. But a host of economists, including a few of his old friends, accused him of having fostered the housing bubble and bust with low interest rates. An even louder chorus of critics blamed him for refusing to clamp down on sleazy mortgage lending. Greenspan, then eighty-one, was having none of it. "There has been an awful lot of selective reporting," he grumbled. "The facts are not as they are presented."

I had been ready to listen quietly. But then he talked about fraud, and I began to feel an irresistible urge to spill my guts. Greenspan was arguing that the bulk of the mortgage fiasco stemmed from criminal fraud—by borrowers, lenders, or both. The Federal Reserve, he insisted, wasn't a criminal investigative agency. "It was up to the legal division," he said with uncharacteristic meekness. Had I interviewed the Fed's general counsel? How about the director of consumer affairs? "Deceptive and unfair practices sound very straightforward, until you try to define them," he said.

What set me off wasn't that the former "maestro" was hiding behind anonymous bureaucrats to justify his inaction; it was the idea that the wave of bad mortgages had resulted from criminals committing fraud. Yes, I had borrowed a huge pile of money without documenting my ability to keep up with the payments. But I hadn't defrauded anybody, and nobody had defrauded me. It had all been perfectly legal. In fact, I had been assisted by a long chain of enablers and promoters—loan officers, underwriters, banks, Wall Street firms, and rating agencies. Blaming the mortgage meltdown on fraud ignored the rot and corruption in the whole system, up to and including policy makers like Greenspan.

"My question isn't about fraud," I interjected. "My question is whether the government should have prevented companies from making big loans to people who couldn't repay them." Then I took a breath. "Let me tell you about my own personal experience with these mortgages."

Greenspan stopped short. He was never comfortable talking about personal issues and seemed to mirror my own discomfort. I might have been the only person he had known personally who had been caught in the mortgage meltdown.

I gave him the short version. In 2004, I had been in the middle of a divorce and was paying out well over half of my take-home pay in child support and alimony. I could barely make ends meet, but I was in love and wanted to get married. To my amazement, I had easily managed to buy a lovely little house in a cozy neighborhood. "It was like a 'don't ask, don't tell' loan," I said. The mortgage company hadn't asked to see my pay stubs or tax returns, and I hadn't told them about the automatic withholdings. They hadn't asked what percentage of my disposable monthly income would go to the mortgage, and I hadn't told them that *all* of it would. They hadn't asked Patty to cosign, and I hadn't told them that she didn't have a job.

The faith-based lending hadn't ended there. Less than two years after buying the house, Patty and I had run up $50,000 in credit card debt. Yet we had been able to refinance the house—not once, but twice—with even bigger mortgages.

I was embarrassed, and Greenspan looked embarrassed for me. But I was trying to make a point: it had all been legal. My mortgage company hadn't cared, because it would sell my loan to Wall Street. The Wall Street firms hadn't cared, because they would bundle the loan into a mortgage-backed security and resell it to investors around the world. The investors hadn't cared, because the rating agencies had given the securities a triple-A rating. And the rating agencies hadn't cared, because their models showed that these loans had performed well in the past.

"Shouldn't the Fed or some other government regulator have stopped them from lending to someone like me?" I asked. Greenspan hated government regulation as much as he loved the free market. The best regulation, he was convinced, was enlightened self-interest.

"Have you defaulted?"

"Not yet. I'm hanging on by my fingernails."

He thought for a moment, and then broke into a wide grin. If I had gone more than three years without defaulting, he said, I had probably validated my lender's calculated risk after all. "They looked at you, saw your steady job history and saw that you had always paid your bills, and they were betting that you would do almost anything to avoid defaulting. And they were right," he said. "I bet they've made money on you already."

Greenspan's initial question had been a fair one. Why did I do it? Why did *we* do it? Why did millions of seemingly sane adults suddenly take leave of their common sense and load up on home mortgages they could not possibly manage? Why did we all jump off the cliff together?

We all had our reasons. Some of us were desperate to fulfill the dream of owning our first home, of arriving in the middle class. Others craved a bigger house, a newer house, a better neighborhood. Still others were dazzled by the seemingly surefire profits from soaring real estate prices.

I had two utterly compelling reasons for taking the plunge. The money was there, and I was in love.

The fever for romance and the speculative fever to get rich have a lot in common. Both are driven by primordial hungers and the allure of once-in-a-lifetime opportunities. Both evolve through a series of escalating gambles. The first is small and cautious—a sly flirtation, or a lowball bid on a condo. But each successful payoff emboldens you to raise the stakes. If the conditions are right, you can escalate very quickly from the harmless flirtation to the languorous dinner, the first kiss, the torrid weekend, and, ultimately, putting your future on the line.

The same can be said for flipping condos in Miami or Las Vegas.

Each winning roll of the dice seems to confirm the strategy and provides more money to raise the stakes. Prudence and patience become dull and petty. If you're on a roll, it's time for big ideas, bold decisions, and heroic leaps of faith. It's all about adventure, danger, and fantasy.

In my case, the twin fevers of romance and housing collided on a glorious Sunday afternoon in April 2004. It was the kind of spring day that was perfect for both lovers and real estate agents. The magnolias and azaleas were ablaze in pink and purple. The young grass was fresh and bright green, and the soft clean breeze felt alive with possibility. On a day like that, even a four-bedroom rambler could look like a dream home.

I had decided on a whim to stroll through some open houses for sale in a modest tree-lined neighborhood in Silver Spring, Maryland. By any ordinary measure, I knew, I could not remotely afford to buy a house. But touring them seemed like a cheap form of entertainment, a harmless bit of voyeurism and fantasy.

At forty-eight, I had separated from my wife after a twenty-one-year marriage and was handing her more than $4,000 a month. I could barely make ends meet in a one-bedroom rental apartment, but I wanted desperately to start a new life with Patty, who was by then my fiancée. She would be moving from Los Angeles to Washington in July, and we would need a home with enough space for ourselves and her two youngest children, as well as for my own boys on the weekends. I had assumed we would start by renting a house or an apartment, but I knew enough about the new breed of mortgages to understand that it was at least theoretically possible to buy something.

The compulsion hit me when I walked into a three-bedroom cottage at the end of a tree-lined lane. The asking price was $400,000, which was low for the area. It was small, but immaculate and homey, and I immediately imagined how it could hold Patty and our mix of children. I felt a rush of sentiment and adrenaline. It was perfect! It was a sign from God. We would buy it, we would love it, and we would be living with our children and each other in our little paradise. I had to have it!

I couldn't afford it, but that didn't mean I couldn't buy it.

I pulled out my cell phone and called the only person I knew who could point me in the right direction—Susan Kilborn, a close friend who was a real estate agent. She gave me the name and number of a mortgage loan officer at American Home Mortgage Corporation named Bob Andrews. Bob wasn't related to me, and I had never heard of the company. "Bob can be very helpful," Susan said. "He specializes in unusual situations."

On a Sunday afternoon, Bob returned my call within minutes. "If we had talked earlier, I could have had you preapproved for a loan in time to make an offer today," he said. He sounded vaguely disappointed, but also wired and ready to jump. "How big a mortgage do you think you'll need?"

"My situation is a little complicated," I warned. I told him about my enormous child support and alimony payments, and said I was banking on Patty to earn enough money to keep us afloat. Bob cut me off. "I specialize in challenges," he said confidently. "As you might imagine, I've got a lot of experience with people going through divorce."

As I quickly found out, American Home Mortgage had become one of the fastest-growing mortgage lenders in the country. It was a rocket of a company, even for the mortgage industry, and would ultimately flame out in a huge bankruptcy in 2007. But none of that mattered right then. It turned out that American Home's specialty was people just like me: borrowers with good credit scores who wanted to stretch their finances far beyond what traditional banks and thrifts would allow. In industry jargon, we were "Alt-A" customers, and we paid slightly higher rates for the privilege of concealing our financial weaknesses.

I thought I knew a lot about the mortgage boom. I had already written several articles for *The New York Times* about the surging growth of both subprime and Alt-A mortgages. I had interviewed people with very modest incomes who had taken out big loans. And though my own experience had been with traditional mortgages, I had owned a house for almost twenty years, had refinanced it twice, and had taken out a home equity line of credit. I had always thought of myself as conservative about borrowing. The mortgage on the first house had been a fifteen-year loan, which cost more per month but would ultimately save tens of thousands of dollars in interest charges.

Nevertheless, I had never really grasped how much had become possible.

Bob called back the next morning. "Your credit scores are almost perfect," he said happily. "Based on your income, you can qualify for a mortgage of about $500,000." That was an eye-opener. I had never contemplated buying a house for a half-million dollars, even before I started surrendering more than half my paycheck to my ex-wife. I was amazed that a company would even contemplate lending that much money to someone in my position, or that a lender simply wouldn't care about the messy details of my life. Bob didn't break a sweat. If I wanted to buy a house, he figured, it was my job to decide whether I could afford it. Once I decided what I wanted, his job was to make it happen.

"I am here to enable dreams," he explained to me long afterward. "If you came to me and said you'd been unemployed for seven years and didn't have a pot to piss in, who am I to tell you that you shouldn't do what you want to do? I am here to sell money, and to help you do what you want to do. At the end of the day, it's your signature on the mortgage—not mine."

You had to admire his muscular logic. My lenders weren't assuming that I was an angel. They were betting that a default would be much more painful to me than to them. If I wanted to take a risk, for whatever reason, they were not going to second-guess me. In fact, money was so cheap and plentiful that they would make it available for almost as little as a conventional mortgage.

What mattered more than anything, Bob explained, was a person's credit record. History seemed to show that the most important predictor of whether people defaulted on their mortgages was their "FICO" score (named after the Fair Isaac Corporation, which had developed the main rating system). Investors had become steadily less interested in the details of a person's financial position. If you had always paid your debts on time before, the theory went, you would probably keep paying on time in the future.

Even if you had a troubled credit history, a huge industry of "subprime" mortgage lenders had arisen to cater to you. Like American Home Mortgage, the subprime lenders relied on complex mathematical models for pricing risk, and incredibly intricate techniques for slicing and dicing that risk. The models showed that defaults on the risky new mortgages were surprisingly low. The models were saying, "Go for it."

In and around Washington DC, home prices had been climbing faster than incomes for so long that even skeptics were capitulating to the excitement by 2004. In trendy suburbs like Bethesda and Chevy Chase, the median home price had doubled since 1998 and hovered around $700,000. Investors there were tearing down three-bedroom split-levels from the early 1960s and replacing them with $2 million mansions. In slightly less affluent, less glamorous areas like Silver Spring, where I was living in a rental apartment, aging four-bedroom houses with small kitchens were selling for $500,000 and up.

I wasn't betting on rising prices. With my luck, I thought, the market would head down the moment I decided to buy anything. What I cared about, passionately, was getting married. Patricia Barreiro was the perfect woman: brainy, regal, sexy, fiery, and eclectic. Best of all, she had been one of my closest friends when we were both innocents at an American high school in Argentina. I was the bookish, unathletic son of an American diplomat, a jumbled mix of sexual awkwardness, intellectual energy, and teenage rebellion. Patty, the daughter of an Argentine doctor and occasional political activist, had been born in Buenos Aires but educated in American schools. She was sexy and cerebral, and she loved talking to me about politics and books at a coffee shop every day after school. We were never romantic, and had gone our separate ways after high school.

Patty was now a mother of four in Los Angeles and had recently endured a bruising divorce after twenty-five years of marriage. At forty-eight, she was still a beauty—statuesque, with green eyes and auburn hair. She had remained a voracious reader, devouring books and newspapers, becoming a trained book editor, and nearly completing a master's degree in Latin American studies by the time of her divorce. But she had become utterly estranged from her husband, a television commercial producer who had become depressed about his work and his life.

My own twenty-one-year marriage had become bitter and quarrelsome and reached the breaking point in 2003. I had just finished a six-year assignment in Germany as the *Times'* European economics correspondent. My ex-wife Julia had liked Europe but resented my workaholic habits and frequent traveling. She complained that

I gave top priority to the newspaper; second priority to our three boys; and last priority to her. She was probably right. I had become snappy and defensive, tired of what felt like a constant power struggle. Even though we were both happy to return to our old house in Washington, our fighting became even more frequent.

I had fallen in love with Patty on a trip through southern California in April 2003. It was the first time in more than twenty years that I had seen her, and she was one of several old friends I was visiting in the area. We talked for hours about what had happened to our lives. She was fascinated by my newspaper work and by the battles raging in Washington. "I'm so happy you were able to find the kind of work that you always wanted," she said. She couldn't understand why Julia resented the long hours or the traveling. Patty could see that I was swooning, but she firmly banished any hopes of something more. She was tired of men, and I was still married. "One thing that won't happen," she wrote me after my visit, "is that you and I become romantic."

But Patty did give me an idea that precipitated the end of my marriage: to cover the war in Iraq. As it happened, I was watching CNN in her living room as US troops entered Baghdad and pulled down the statue of Saddam Hussein. "You should have your editors send you to Iraq," she told me. "You'd be perfect, because the story will be about economic reconstruction." I scoffed at first, but she persisted and I began to fixate on the idea myself. I was restless for some adventure, unhappy about my marriage, and unable to see any way of being with Patty. "Fine," I told her. "If I can't have love, then I'll take the war." Wasn't that why men had joined the French foreign legion?

As it turned out, the editors at the paper were eager to relieve the exhausted reporters who had covered the invasion. They told me to pack my bags as fast as I could. Julia was enraged, vowing to make me sleep in the basement when I returned, and possibly move out entirely. I didn't care. Deep inside, her threat made me happy. Iraq was the biggest story of my life and one that would tap almost every kind of skill I had as a reporter. Our boys—Ryan, 14; and 12-year-old twins Matthew and Daniel—were initially frightened at the prospect, but they relaxed as I explained that the job would not be as dangerous as they thought.

Less than three weeks after I had seen Patty in Los Angeles, I arrived at the Palestine Hotel in Baghdad and began a two-month stint as a war correspondent. I wrote her constantly to describe what I was seeing and experiencing in Iraq. We didn't talk much about romance, though the undercurrent was always there. I wrote in the afternoons and evenings from Baghdad, and she would read my emails in Los Angeles each morning. At one point, Patty warned me that I should stop writing if I thought I was jeopardizing my marriage. I reluctantly broke off communication for several weeks, but I was so miserable that I soon resumed.

By the time I returned to Washington in July, my marriage was all but over. Julia, still furious that I had jumped into a war zone, made good on her promise and ordered me to sleep in the basement. I was relieved to be sleeping on my own. I was tired of defending myself, torn by my emotional conflicts and longing for love. I would have gladly stayed in Iraq for several more months, but I had missed my boys.

"Don't you want to be a better person?" Julia asked me, during a meeting with our marriage counselor after I got back. "No," I said, surprising even myself. "I want to be a happier person."

A few weeks later, Julia got her hands on a raft of my emails to Patty. It was clear that we hadn't so much as kissed, but it was also clear that I had become far closer to Patty than to my wife. "You have to stop communicating with her," Julia demanded. If I didn't, she warned, I would have to move out of the house and the marriage would be over. She was right. I told her I couldn't or wouldn't break off my contact with Patty. I didn't have the heart for my marriage anymore. I had to get out, whatever the price might be. I moved out the next day.

Even though I had no idea how we could overcome the practical hurdles, I was already convinced that I wanted to spend the rest of my life with Patty. We poured out our feelings in long conversations on the telephone, night after night. She had touched my soul in ways I couldn't explain and couldn't really understand. Between my memories of the friendship we had shared as teenagers and the sad warmth that she radiated today, she was like a salvation to me. I asked her to marry me even before going out to visit her in person a few weeks later.

"You are the woman I want to grow old with," I told her. "I'm as certain about it as anything I have been before." Even in the delirium of the moment, that pronouncement took Patty aback. But she didn't need much persuading. "I love you and I cannot wait to be married to you," she responded, sounding as if she were experiencing something joyful for the first time in years. Over Labor Day weekend of 2003, I flew to Los Angeles and kissed Patty for the first time. We continued to live on separate coasts another year, flying back and forth for visits every month or so. By the spring of 2004, we were making plans for her to move east with her two youngest children in the summer and trying to figure out how we were going to pull it off with our limited resources.

Patty and I were complements—a "perfect fit," she liked to say. She had always liked men who were brainy and even nerdy. "I don't care what a man looks like, as long as he's smart," she said. To her, I was a refreshing change from the men she had known in Los Angeles. I didn't care much about money or expensive cars. I dressed modestly and, at least at first glance, I didn't seem to be an overbearing, self-absorbed macho. From what she could see, working at the *Times* was a bit like working at a university: fascinating and creative—an environment without much money but filled with very smart people. From my vantage point, Patty was a kindred spirit who also possessed things I could only imagine: an encyclopedic knowledge about fashion, literature, and pop culture; a passion for food; a shrewd but sympathetic awareness of the chemistry between men and women.

———————

In the days and weeks following that glorious Sunday afternoon of house hunting in April 2004, I felt as if I had walked into a no-limit game of Texas hold 'em. Armed with my "lender's letter" from Bob declaring that American Home was ready to lend me up to $500,000, I sat down with Susan, our real estate agent, to make an offer on the sweet little cottage for $400,000. "Don't even think about offering less than the asking price," Susan said. Fine, I agreed. "Do you want to make the offer conditional on the results of a home inspection?" she asked me. Sure, I said. Why commit myself to a house that might have a crack in the roof, right? But Susan recommended against that. Sellers wanted as few complications as possible.

Offering the full price, with or without conditions, was no guarantee, of course. Other home buyers had included "escalator" clauses in their offers—mechanisms that automatically raised their bids if any rival offered the same amount. If rival buyers had escalator clauses, they set off an instant bidding war until all but one of the escalators had reached its preauthorized limit. Within hours, I learned that the sweet little cottage had sold for $20,000 more than the asking price.

Sobered, I bid on a second house several weeks later. Once again, I met the seller's asking price of $400,000. But this time, I added an escalator clause to raise the bid as much as $20,000. Once again, I was outbid.

Three months after making my first unsuccessful bid for a house, Patty arrived in Washington, in July 2004. Flying in several weeks ahead of her children, who were staying with their father, she plunged straight into house hunting. She and Susan scouted all the neighborhoods within moderately close proximity of my old house, so that my boys could stay close to me and travel easily between our house and the house that I had turned over to my ex-wife. Patty and Susan began by looking at rental houses. Most of them were what they came to call "icky"—run-down, depressing, and expensive. Some looked like they had been lived in by either college students or drug dealers. We quickly reverted to searching for houses to buy.

After weeks of looking, Patty and Susan discovered a small but stately brick home in a leafy, kid-filled neighborhood called Wood-moor, in Silver Spring. The house had four tiny bedrooms and the owner wanted $480,000. But there was no central air-conditioning—a big negative in the former swamp known as Washington—and the house had been on the market for several weeks. The owner had moved to take a job in a different city, and he was unusually open to offers.

I was so busy at the time that I hadn't actually seen the house, but I trusted Patty and Susan and sent in an offer of $460,000. One day later, we got our answer: the sellers had accepted. Not only that, but Susan had persuaded them to let us move in almost immediately, and to rent the house from them until the closing later in August. I felt both amazed and exhilarated, convinced that the stars had aligned for us. I loved the house as soon as I saw it. It was one block from a school and a park. My boys would be within a fifteen-minute drive, and it would be easy for them to come over and stay whenever they wanted. And we would be far less cramped here than in my old apartment. Best of all, we would be ready to move in just a day or two after Patty's children arrived.

Bob Andrews jumped into action immediately, and I quickly began to learn the intricacies of "don't ask, don't tell" lending.

Bob's original plan had been to write two mortgages, one for 80 percent of the purchase price and a piggyback loan for 10 percent. I would kick in the final 10 percent, cashing out a chunk of *New York Times* stock—my last. If I had been a normal borrower, the whole deal would have sailed through at a low interest rate. My $130,000 salary and my assets were easy to document. Even by the conservative guidelines for traditional fixed-rate mortgages, my gross monthly income would have been enough to qualify for a monthly "nut"— the mortgage payment, plus a month's worth of property taxes and property insurance, totaling $3,000 a month. But given my actual income after alimony and child support, I couldn't possibly qualify for a standard mortgage. In the parlance of mortgage lenders, my "back-end ratio"—the ratio of my income minus existing financial obligations—was almost 100 percent. No banker would sign off on a back-end ratio higher than about 50 percent. Bob's plan was to write a "stated-income loan," or "liar's loan," so that I wouldn't have to give the game away by producing paychecks or tax returns.

The liar's loan was amazingly cheap. In exchange for agreeing not to verify my income, American Home Mortgage would notch up my interest rate by about one-quarter of a percent. That was only a guess, because mortgage lenders didn't disclose how much they had added to the basic interest rate to accommodate special risk factors. The fees could add almost $1,000 a year to my mortgage bill. The only logical reason for people to pay the extra

money was to exaggerate their incomes, so it seemed like a semiof-
ficial encouragement for people to lie. I wasn't about to complain.
Whatever extra fees I might be swallowing in the form of higher
interest rates, the rate itself on the interest-only loan was only 5.6
percent and wouldn't adjust for five years.

Unfortunately, Bob's plan hit a snag a few days later. "Ed, the
underwriters say that your name is on another mortgage," he told
me. "That means you're carrying too much debt."

The mortgage was on my old house, which I had turned over to
my ex-wife. As part of our separation agreement, which I quickly
faxed to Bob, she had accepted full legal responsibility for making
the payments. But once again, I wasn't a normal borrower. The
separation agreement also spelled out exactly how much I had to
pay each month to my ex-wife. If we showed it to the underwriters, they would see how much I was required to pay out in child
support and alimony. They wouldn't have any problem with the
mortgage on my old house, but they would reject me because of
my child support and alimony payments.

Once again, Bob did not let himself get flustered. If plan A hadn't
worked, he would simply move down another step on the ladder of
credibility. Instead of taking out a "stated-income loan," I wouldn't
bother to state any income at all. It was absurd, but it was true. It
was called a "no-ratio" mortgage, and it meant that American Home
Mortgage would verify only my assets (mainly the cash I had from
selling my stock). Since I was not even stating my income, the lender
wouldn't care about my debt-to-income ratio. It wouldn't matter
whether I was on the hook for a second mortgage or not.

American Home seemed to be colluding with me to pull the
wool over its own eyes. Why bother with income requirements at
all if you knew full well a borrower couldn't meet them?

As much as I thought I knew about mortgages, I was only obliquely aware of everything that was happening. I knew my total monthly payments would be about $2,500 a month for the first five years. After that, my interest rate and monthly payments on the first mortgage would adjust every year and would probably jump even if overall interest rates were almost unchanged. I wouldn't have known even that much if Bob hadn't personally explained how the formula for the adjustable interest rate would work. But even then, I had very little idea of how much I was paying in hidden fees that were rolled into my interest rate, or how much they might end up costing me five years down the road.

If I had investigated, I would have been surprised at what I learned. By any measure, I was paying 5.625 percent on my primary mortgage of $333,700. That was pretty low, given all the obvious machinations to avoid documenting my income. But I was also paying a sky-high rate of 8.5 percent on my second, "piggyback" loan for $80,300, and I would face a balloon payment for the full remaining amount of principal after ten years. It was easy to imagine the monthly payments jumping about 25 percent, or $600 a month on the first mortgage. If my monthly rate jumped by 2 percentage points to 7.625 from 5.625, which was entirely possible given that interest rates were at almost historic lows in 2004, my monthly interest payment on the first mortgage would jump from $1,579 plus taxes and insurance to $2,363. On top of that, I would have to start paying the principal on my loan. That would add another $130 a month.

"So even if interest rates don't increase at all, I would end up paying more each month?" I asked Bob, shortly before I signed the huge pile of papers to close the deal on my house. "Don't worry," Bob answered, adding what almost everybody else in real estate was saying at that moment. "The value of your house will be higher in five years. You'll be able to refinance."

2

PRUDENCE IS FOR LOSERS

To Alan Greenspan, not to mention every real estate agent, home builder, and mortgage broker in the country, the word *bubble* was taboo in 2004.

In Washington, almost nobody saw anything ominous about soaring home prices. Real estate was the main reason that the recession in 2001 had been as mild as it had been, and the reason that household wealth had bounced back to new highs afterward. Increases in wealth usually produced increases in consumer spending even if incomes were stagnant, and Americans were holding true to form. Thanks to the boom in home equity loans and lines of credit, people were treating their houses like ATM machines. Consumer spending kept climbing through the recession of 2001 and the sluggish period of job losses and stubbornly high unemployment.

Even in 2004, though, a handful of prescient economists were warning that a speculative bubble in housing prices had already formed. Three weeks before Patty and I signed our mortgage papers in late August 2004, Merrill Lynch published an early warning about the housing market by its chief North American economist, David Rosenberg. Lest anybody miss his point, the report's cover featured giant bubbles floating in front of a McMansion. "Are those bubbles coming from my backyard?" asked the caption.

Using a raft of data, Rosenberg argued that housing prices were wildly out of sync with fundamental values. The gap between the cost of owning and renting had widened to an all-time record. History showed that the bigger the gap, known as the price-rent ratio, the more likely home prices were set to flatten out or even decline.

Home prices also had shot up much faster than Americans' ability to pay for them. Interest rates were at their lowest levels in a half century, and yet housing had become much less affordable. Americans were bridging the shortfall by borrowing more heavily and spending a bigger share of their take-home pay on mortgage payments. "First-time buyers have strapped on so much debt that roughly one-third now pay at least 30 percent of their after-tax income on shelter (and half of the lowest income households spend at least 50 percent of their incomes on housing)," Rosenberg noted. It wasn't sustainable. If home prices kept climbing faster than income, it wouldn't be long before families hit the wall.

Rosenberg's warnings would turn out to be deadly accurate. But in retrospect, what made them striking was that Merrill Lynch's top executives disregarded them entirely. As an economic voice, you might say, Merrill Lynch was courageously and almost constantly warning the public that the United States was dangerously overextended. But in the real world, where Merrill Lynch was making billions of dollars in profits on exotic mortgage-backed securities, it was trying to torque up those winnings by using vast amounts of borrowed money.

In the world of economics and accounting, the ironclad logic of prices, incomes, and the rough balance between assets and liabilities left no doubt that the US housing market had either become a speculative bubble already or would become one very soon. As we had all learned from the dot-com stock mania, a speculative bubble pumped up only by the belief that prices will climb higher will eventually pop. The bigger the bubble, the bigger the bust. But like Merrill Lynch, people were making their decisions in the real world. And the evidence that they used to value a house was based on what they saw and heard, as well as what Adam Smith called the "invisible hand" of supply and demand.

The pressures weren't rational or irrational; they were just there. It might be the young couple who just outbid you for what seemed like an overpriced starter house. Maybe it was a friend from high school who bought two condos with no money down and resold them both for a hefty profit. Or maybe it was that guy at work—the well-coifed one whose shirts never wrinkled and who never seemed to be stressed—who had bought a glamorous house with a risky mortgage and seemed to be having the time of his life. If everybody around you was paying crazy prices, how crazy could the prices be?

It made me feel like Smith's invisible-hand puppet. I knew we had paid 37 percent more for our house than the previous owners had paid two years earlier. I didn't think for one minute that it would be a good investment, but I was as much a part of the frenzy as anybody else. I might not be one of the condo flippers, and I might not be expecting to make any money, but I was doing just as much as they were to inflate the bubble.

But what about Alan Greenspan and his army of economists at the Federal Reserve? Those people were being paid to look at numbers and think analytically about risk. They were supposed to be on the alert for potential train wrecks before they occurred. Yet

most of them ignored the compelling evidence and dismissed complaints that twin speculative bubbles had formed in both housing
prices and mortgage lending.

It was a strange attitude, given that the United States had just
experienced the traumatic collapse of the technology stock bubble.
Yet Greenspan and Ben S. Bernanke, who would succeed Greenspan as Fed chairman, both argued at length that it was point-
less to try to pop bubbles before they burst. They also argued
that the Fed's only method of pricking one was to jack up interest
rates—a move that had the potential to drive the economy into a
recession.

Even I surrendered to the cautious conventional wisdom in an
article I wrote in June 2004 about the explosive growth in risky
mortgages. "Most analysts agree that there is no nationwide housing bubble because housing prices have climbed only slowly in the
Midwest and the South, even as they have soared on the East and
West coasts," I wrote.

There seemed to be something else going on. Nobody at the
Fed or in the Bush administration was sounding any alarms about
speculative excesses in subprime and Alt-A loans. At the same
time, they certainly warned about the things they did care about—
antismoking campaigns; drug awareness programs; the wicked
twins Fannie Mae and Freddie Mac, which Greenspan and Bush
both viewed as dangerous remnants of the New Deal and the era
of "Big Government." But issue warnings that you risked destroying your retirement by buying a house you couldn't comfortably
afford? No way.

Bush had actually created a new government-sponsored, no-
money-down deal called the American Dream Downpayment
Fund. Bush's proudest economic accomplishment, he made clear,
was that his tax cuts of 2001 and 2003 would lower taxes by more

than a trillion dollars over ten years. He took almost as much pride in positioning himself as a champion of the "ownership society." Particularly during the long period during Bush's first term when jobs were disappearing month after month—long after the recession had officially ended—the president and his top officials boasted that the home ownership rate had edged up to a new record of 69.2 percent by 2004.

The housing market didn't need any help from the government. Over most of the past century, home prices climbed only about 1 percentage point a year faster than inflation, according to research by Robert J. Shiller of Yale University. But starting in 1998, nationwide housing prices began climbing at a pace that wildly outstripped historical patterns. "Real" home prices, adjusted for inflation, climbed 52 percent from 2000 to 2004. Meanwhile, the real median household income had been almost flat during the same period. By 2004, the trend had gone on too long to dismiss as a routine aberration.

Shiller studied behavioral economics, a field that often made other economists queasy because it looked at how irrational, psychological factors could play a central role in economic behavior. Shiller didn't talk much about interest rates or income growth. He talked about the stories people told each other, and about the chatter that dominated cocktail parties. To many economists, this approach seemed flaky and kooky. Nevertheless, Shiller had accurately predicted the collapse of the dot-com bubble before it happened. By early 2005, he had concluded that the housing market posed an even bigger and more dangerous bubble than tech stocks had.

Other researchers agreed with Shiller. "Affordability went bust during the housing boom," remarked Desmond Lachman, a scholar at the American Enterprise Institute in Washington. Lachman had drawn up a chart that showed exactly what happened. From 1979

until 2000, home prices hovered around 3.2 times the median family income. But starting in 2000, the ratio jumped to more than 4.
These were abstract numbers and ratios—but they provided cold,
clear evidence of increasingly self-destructive behavior.

Home buyers were taking on obligations that were bigger than
they had any valid reason to think they could repay. Investors were
pouring money into steadily riskier mortgages without being able
to explain why they expected outsized returns. Both were engag-
ing in the logic of chain letters and Ponzi schemes: their bets
would pay off because other people behind them would buy them
out by placing bigger bets, and others behind them would raise
the bidding even higher. It was tempting to argue that the world
had always worked this way, and it was true that home prices had
climbed year after year for decades. The crucial difference, though,
was that home prices hadn't climbed much faster than inflation or
inflation-adjusted incomes.

In the abstract, it was hard to see how home buyers wouldn't hit
a wall. In the real world, where things were bigger and more complicated and more hormonal than in any model, it was hard not to
go with the herd. To be sure, there were logical economic reasons
why housing prices had kept soaring. The big one was plunging
interest rates, which had drastically reduced the cost of owning a
home. To prop up economic growth during and after the recession
of 2001, the Federal Reserve had slashed the cost of borrowing
money to its lowest level since the 1950s. Cheaper money meant
lower mortgage payments. Lower payments meant that people
could afford more expensive homes. With the economy growing at
a seemingly healthy pace and unemployment heading down, why
hold back?

I realized just how fixated people had become on rising home
prices at an end-of-summer block party, a month after we moved

into our house. A neighbor named Mike asked me how much we had paid for our home. Mike had lived on the street for more than a decade and had no plans of moving. But when I told him we had paid $460,000, he seemed momentarily disappointed. "You don't have central air-conditioning," he remarked, almost to himself. I could see him doing mental calculations about what our purchase price implied about his house across the street, and our lack of air-conditioning seemed to reassure him. I realized that many of our neighbors had probably toured our house while it was on the market and made mental notes about the number, size, and state of repair of our bathrooms and bedrooms. They were constantly reestimating the value of their own properties, almost as nervously as they might have been checking the price of their shares in America Online back in 2000.

Several months after the party, a young couple with children in the same kindergarten as our daughter sold their house for $625,000. The perky price was hot news among the parents at the school bus stop. We all congratulated the mother, and silently congratulated ourselves. It had been only three years since the dot-com implosion had wiped out trillions of dollars in wealth along with the rhetoric about a "new paradigm" and a "new economy." One might have thought that people would be nervous about anything resembling the previous mania. Yet there we were: buying into an even newer idea of permanently soaring property prices. We were spending more and more of our income on real estate, either buying new houses or expanding the ones we had. And we were borrowing more and more of the money to carry it off, leaving smaller and smaller margins for error. It was an impossible trend. If housing prices kept climbing faster than household incomes, people wouldn't have enough money left over for anything else they wanted. Something had to give.

But not just yet. For the time being, housing prices had become disconnected from people's ability to pay. The *Think and Grow Rich!* speculators assumed that prices would keep surging. The more desperate middle-class strivers were afraid prices would keep surging. For all the intricacy of the new go-go mortgages, the one common thread was that almost all of them allowed people to postpone the full cost of borrowing for two to ten years.

"It was play now, pay later," said William Tessar, a veteran mortgage broker in Calabasas, California. Everybody in the mortgage business knew that exotic loans were the hottest part of the market. Interest-only loans, no-money-down loans, and "pay option" loans that allowed borrowers to pay even less than the minimum interest were both more profitable and easier to sell than traditional fixed-rate mortgages.

As is so often the case in trend setting, southern California not only epitomized the housing mania but had also led the way in pioneering subprime mortgages. Just a few months before buying my house, I spent several days in Los Angeles and Orange County to see firsthand the cutting edge of the mortgage market. Southern California had one of the most overheated housing markets in the country, but what made it important to the rest of the country was that it was also the home of exotic mortgages.

Orange County, particularly the corridor running from Anaheim down through Irvine and Costa Mesa, had given birth to many of the biggest subprime lenders: New Century Financial, Ditech Funding, Ameriquest, Option One, Long Beach Mortgage. Entrepreneurial and flamboyant, these were banks and finance companies that specialized in charging high fees and high interest rates to borrowers with low incomes, low credit scores, or little cash. In some cases, they loaned money to people with higher incomes who wanted to take higher risks. Companies like Ditech and First Franklin developed some of the first no-money-down mortgages. Long Beach Mortgage had been one of the early developers of "option ARM" mortgages, also known as "pick-a-payment" loans, which allowed borrowers to make less than the minimum interest payment and rack up more debt each month.

Southern California provided an ideal environment for what had once been called "creative financing." Housing prices were among the highest in the country, meaning that people often had to stretch their incomes. The region had a long tradition of real estate booms and busts, a lot of discretionary money, and a big concentration of entrepreneurs and people tied to the entertainment industry whose fortunes swung wildly from one year to the next. By necessity and cultural inclination, home buyers and lenders alike had a tradition of taking risks and experimenting with unorthodox financial arrangements.

I loved southern California, with its sunny weather, its easy drive to beaches and mountains, and its high concentration of people who seemed tanned and rich. I took guilty pleasure in watching the people who flaunted their wealth by driving sporty Mercedes convertibles with the tops down. Men didn't wear ties; women wore spiky heels. What wasn't to like? And you had to appreciate the openness to entrepreneurial creativity: people in California were good at coming up with new ideas and building businesses from scratch. It was no wonder that they were also masters of creative financing.

They had to be. The median price for a single-family home in Orange County had hit $572,000 at that point, up 28 percent in just one year and nearly double what it had been just three years earlier. These were not mansions in Bel Air or Beverly Hills, or beachside cottages in San Diego or La Jolla. These were mass-built tract homes in sprawling new developments, bedroom communities in which people often had hour-long commutes to work.

Ladera Ranch, launched in 1999 in the dry, grassy hills near Mission Viejo, contained thousands of homes and was adding hundreds more each year. Looking out from a ridge on one side, you could see taupe-colored houses for miles. The models had names like "Segovia" and "Encantada," and the builders said they blended architectural styles like "European Cottage," "Spanish Revival," "French Revival," and "San Juan Rustic."

Demand for the homes was so high that thousands of people were on waiting lists, some of them for nearly a year, just for the chance to sign a contract to buy a house about to be built. When one builder announced that he would hold an online registration for several dozen new lots, he had so many buyers that the sign-up was over in less than fifteen minutes. Another builder held a lottery to sell off about a hundred parcels reserved for custom-built homes priced at $1 million and up. About two thousand people showed up, each bringing a check for $10,000 in earnest money in case they won.

Prices were climbing with such speed that shrewd speculators could flip properties for a big profit before the house had been finished. In an area known as Sutter's Mill, Centex Homes raised the price of its three-bedroom townhouses from $377,990 in early 2004 to $496,890 by the end of the year.

Orange County was literally becoming too expensive for most of its inhabitants. According to the California Association of Realtors, only 27 percent of families in the county earned enough money at that time to qualify for a traditional thirty-year fixed mortgage on a median-priced single-family house. And that was assuming a borrower had been able to make a 20 percent down payment. Builders and real estate agents told me that prices were rising because southern California had an acute shortage of land. The population was climbing, they added, and environmental restrictions were shrinking the supply of buildable land.

All that was true, but it didn't explain the mania. Land had been scarce for years in Orange County, and California had a long history of imposing tough restrictions on land use. The supply of land might be tight, but it hadn't changed that much in three years. What had changed was the demand for houses, and demand was being driven at least partly by a state of mind. "It was crazy," said Lupita Lamitie, a mortgage broker who bought a townhouse in Ladera Ranch in 2004. "You felt that if you didn't buy right then, prices were going to be even higher if you waited."

Eric Falcinella, a sales executive in his early thirties, bought a condo at Ladera Ranch for $395,000 in 2004. He had been so eager to buy that he had signed up on the waiting list for a condo as soon as the builder, MBK Homes, had started taking names one year earlier. Not only did he borrow 100 percent of the purchase price, which meant he was starting out with no equity in the home, but he took out an interest-only loan that would not pay down any of his principal. Even so, the monthly payments, including taxes and condominium fees, added up to a hefty $3,400 a month. "Sure I'm worried," he told me, shortly after he bought his condo. "But I'm figuring that my income will go up and that the house will go up in value."

Virginia Carlson, a loan officer with Countrywide Financial who worked on-site at Ladera Ranch, told me that 60 percent of the buyers were getting interest-only loans and borrowing 100 percent of the purchase price. "They want to keep their money in the bank," Carlson said. "They know that six months from now, they are probably going to gain 30 percent equity in their house."

Southern California was more extreme than most other parts of the country, but it wasn't unique. The nation's biggest banks and financial companies were either swooping in to buy up Orange County's subprime lenders or copying their ideas shamelessly. Either way, they were rolling out the ideas on a nationwide basis. Washington Mutual bought Long Beach Mortgage, one of the very oldest subprime lenders. Lehman Brothers, the Wall Street investment bank, built up a full-service subprime lending operation, starting with its acquisition of BNC Lending in Irvine. General Motors Acceptance Corporation, the financing subsidiary of General Motors, bought Ditech. H&R Block, the nationwide tax preparation company, bought Option One. And Countrywide Financial, the nation's biggest mortgage lender, started a subprime lending business in 2003, trumpeting its "fast and easy" low-doc mortgages and jumping into every other variant of high-risk loan that became trendy as well.

To speed up their geographic expansions, the go-go lenders recruited armies of independent mortgage brokers around the country. The independent brokers faced the same underwriting requirements as in-house loan officers, but their sales pitches and explanations of how loans worked came under far less supervision from the lender. The independent brokers often had roots in local communities, giving them entrée to clusters of immigrants and ethnic minorities who had been ignored by mainstream banks.

In a little-noticed anomaly, it was far easier for people to become registered and licensed as mortgage brokers than it was to become licensed as stockbrokers or even insurance agents. But for many of their customers, mortgage brokers were at the center of transactions involving hundreds of thousands of dollars each and big shares of a family's wealth.

The bottom line was a huge increase in the amount of money that people could borrow against their homes. Whitney Tilson, founder of T2 Partners, an investment firm in New York, estimated that borrowing power for a home buyer with an income of $30,000 a year doubled from 1995 through 2004. By far the biggest reason for that increase in borrowing power was the rise of interest-only and no-money-down loans.

People like me could mix and match the offerings almost any way we wanted. What began as specialized programs—no-doc loans for self-employed people; subprime loans for people with poor credit; "pay-option" loans for people who wanted low initial payments; or no-money-down loans for people who didn't have up-front cash—were increasingly being combined into Frankenstein loans that combined all of the nightmarish features at once.

"The mortgage industry is built on three legs," said Paul Reddam, the founder of Ditech Funding, a major subprime lender before he sold it to General Motors' financial arm in 1999. "The first is a person's ability to pay. The second is a person's willingness to pay. And the third is the amount of collateral a person is willing to put up. People began to realize that you could knock out one of those legs, charge a higher interest rate and still have a very good business. What happened is that they started knocking out all three legs at the same time."

Ditech was a pioneer in eliminating the requirement for collateral. Traditional lenders required people to provide 20 percent of the purchase price up front. Ditech not only offered loans without any down payment; it offered to lend people 125 percent of the estimated value of their house. That meant borrowers would initially owe more than the purchase price of their homes. Scores of other companies offered piggyback loans like the one I used to buy my house. These loans went on top of a first mortgage and made it possible for people to buy a house with no money down.

No-doc and low-doc loans undermined the safety that comes from knowing a person's ability to repay. And subprime loans, created for people with checkered credit histories, undermined the certainty about a person's willingness to repay.

Thanks to the Federal Reserve, which had reduced its benchmark interest rate to just 1 percent, mortgage rates were at historic lows in 2004. The smart move for most people would have been to lock in those low rates with an old-fashioned thirty-year fixed-rate mortgage. But that wasn't happening. Home prices were climbing so rapidly that a growing percentage of families couldn't afford to buy with a traditional fixed-rate mortgage.

The result was bizarre: the volume of fixed-rate mortgages, the kind you most want to have when interest rates are low, were actually plunging. Fixed-rate mortgages accounted for 62.3 percent of all new mortgages in 2003, but that share would drop to just 33.2 percent by 2006. By contrast, the volume of Alt-A mortgages shot up from $60 billion in 2001 to $200 billion in 2004, according to *Inside Mortgage Finance,* an industry journal. Subprime lending exploded even more, climbing from $190 billion in 2001 to $540 billion in 2004.

Despite the evidence of a price bubble, and the increase in go-go mortgage lending, neither Alan Greenspan nor most policy makers in the Bush administration saw reason to worry. Speaking at a meeting of the American Economic Association in January 2004, Greenspan brushed aside doubt. "My own sense is that we don't have to worry too much about the emergence of real bubbles again for a while because I think it takes a number of years for the trauma of the collapse to wear off."

Greenspan had been an assiduous student of the housing market long before it became cool to be one. He knew that low interest rates could stimulate the economy through the housing market. He also knew that a housing boom affects more than just the construction industry, furniture makers, or appliance manufacturers. People could cash out some of the value in their existing homes and use the equity to finance vacations, new cars, and investment in start-up businesses. That was exactly what Greenspan had hoped to accomplish when the Fed started slashing interest rates in 2001. With the collapse of the dot-com bubble and the uncertainty after the terrorist attacks of September 11, it was clear that business investment would be flat for quite a while and that consumers would have to carry the day.

Greenspan and the Fed seemed determined to squelch warnings about a housing bubble. In December 2004, the Federal Reserve Bank of New York published an essay by two senior economists who dismissively rejected arguments by those who raised alarms about skyrocketing prices. "A close analysis of the U.S. housing market in recent years," wrote Richard W. Peach and Jonathan McCarthy, "finds little basis for such concerns." Far from being the result of a speculative mania, they continued, "the marked upturn in home prices is largely attributable to market fundamentals." Indeed, they said, the rise in prices was in line with the rise in incomes and the decline in interest rates. Yet even their analysis showed—in a vivid graph, no less—that home prices had climbed more than twice as much during this boom than in either of the two previous housing booms in the 1970s and '80s.

One analyst who loudly and consistently defied the conventional wisdom was Dean Baker, codirector of the Center for Economic and Policy Research, a left-leaning economic research group in Washington. As early as 2002, Baker pointed out that the cost of

owning a home had climbed sharply higher than the cost of renting—a statistic that David Rosenberg would cite in his 2004 report
for Merrill Lynch. Baker also noted that spending on housing was
taking up a bigger and bigger share of people's total consumption;
and like Robert Shiller, he noted that the run-up in housing prices
since 1998 had no precedent in the period since World War II and
defied plausible explanation.

In 2003, Baker grew even more adamant and warned that home
ownership, far from being the American dream, might well be
the fast path to poverty. "While home ownership may indeed be
desirable in normal times, it is not clear that encouraging mod-
erate income families to buy homes at present is good strategy,"
he wrote. Noting that housing prices had already risen 30 percent
above the general increase in consumer prices, he warned that "it
is entirely reasonable to believe that the price of these homes could
fall 30 percent or more when the housing market returns to a more
sustainable path."

At the time, I thought Baker was overstating the doomsday scenario. But I thought he was closer to the truth than Greenspan or
almost anybody in the Bush administration, which had turned the
"ownership society" into a campaign theme for the 2004 reelec-
tion. Every month, White House press flacks would roll out the
latest home ownership figures as proof that Americans were doing
better than ever.

Karl Rove, Bush's political strategist, was convinced that the
expanding "ownership society" provided a powerful opportunity
for Republicans to benefit from a rise in pro-business sentiments.
Rove argued that the shift of Americans toward individual retirement accounts—IRAs and 401(k)'s—had turned the United States
into a nation of investors who would think like pro-business Republicans. It was the same thing with home owners. Home owners

cared about raising families, putting down roots, and investing for the future. They were instinctively conservative and pro-business, which Rove thought offered a huge advantage for Republicans.

Dean Baker thought it was hogwash, and he was ready to put money on it. Shortly before I bought my house, he told me he had put his money where his mouth was: he and his wife had sold their two-bedroom condominium in Washington for $445,000 and were moving into a rental apartment of comparable quality. The rent would be $2,200 a month, which was more than he had been paying on his $160,000 mortgage. But given everything he had been preaching about the housing bubble, he had decided he should get out of the condo while the getting was good.

Baker's friends told him he was throwing away money. Condo prices were surging in Washington, especially in his hotly-sought neighborhood just north of Dupont Circle. In addition, they warned him, he would be losing the valuable mortgage tax break. But Baker, a bearded and bearish man, had been warning so loudly about the housing bubble that he couldn't stand the thought of being hammered by the very bust that he had been predicting.

When Baker told me his news, he sounded more elated than I had ever heard him before. I listened, feeling chagrin and foreboding. I congratulated Baker on his willingness to buck the crowd, and I meant it. But I didn't have the nerve to admit that I was doing exactly the opposite of what he had done. Not only was I buying a house near the peak of the market; I was doing it with an interest-only loan and taking the biggest gamble of my life.

3

MY LENDER
DRINKS THE KOOL-AID

As I walked out of the settlement office with my loan papers, I couldn't shake the sense of having just done something bad . . . but also kind of cool.

My parents would have been horrified. During the entire time they were married, they had bought one and only one house, for $35,000. My late father had worked as a diplomat and been through his share of adventures, but he and my mother were utterly boring about money, avoiding risks and paying all their bills on time. They had never run up credit card debt, refinanced the mortgage, or borrowed against the ballooning value of the house. Their monthly house payments had never climbed above $500, and my mother had paid off the mortgage years earlier. Compared to my parents, I was the prodigal son who was just about to blow his inheritance.

At the same time, I was amazed by how easy it had been. I had just come up with a *half-million dollars,* and I hadn't broken a sweat. It was more than three times as much money as I made in a year, a head-spinning amount if I had been able to spend it however I liked. It was enough to live for years on a remote beach without working. If I had been told to spend it all on cars and luxury consumer goods, I wouldn't have known how to get through half of it. Yet the whole effort had probably taken less than four hours of work on my part. I couldn't help feeling like a high roller, a sophisticated player who could lay his hands on big money at a moment's notice. I had whipped through the pile of loan documents with élan in less than forty-five minutes. Even though it was all about buying a house in the suburbs, it felt vaguely exciting, edgy, and a little gangsta.

But who was the man behind my money? I figured he had to be a real player, a true high roller who knew how to live on the edge.

Michael J. Strauss, the founder and chief executive of American Home Mortgage, was far less well known than industry buccaneers like Angelo Mozilo, the Bronx-born chief executive of Countrywide Financial. Despite his relative obscurity, Strauss had already made his mark as a hotshot. He had started American Home Mortgage as a one-man company in his Manhattan apartment in 1988, when he was all of twenty-nine years old. In 2003, *Fortune* magazine named American Home the second-fastest-growing company in the United States. By the time I signed my loan papers in August 2004, the company was originating $23 billion in mortgages a year—almost a half-billion dollars a week—and it would more than double that number by 2007. Based in a huge glass-and-steel headquarters in Melville, New York, Strauss employed almost four thousand people around the country in 2004, and that workforce would swell to more than seven thousand by 2007.

I thought Strauss might be similar to the subprime pioneers from southern California. Paul Reddam, the onetime professor of philosophy who had founded Ditech Funding, had become famous for his Ferraris and his thoroughbred racehorses. Roland Arnall, the billionaire founder of Ameriquest, had become one of California's biggest philanthropists and a major political contributor. President George W. Bush nominated Arnall to be ambassador to the Netherlands just as a task force of state attorneys general was investigating Ameriquest for deceptive lending practices.

On some level you had to appreciate the mortgage buccaneers. They introduced both democracy and demagoguery to the mortgage business, advertising on late-night television to people who had been shunned by traditional banks and thrifts. They catered to borrowers with tarnished credit and erratic incomes. They attracted millions of customers who had never owned a home—a disproportionate share of whom were African-American, Latino, or other minorities.

The new breed had honed a new gospel of lending that was spreading to the entire industry: (1) no borrower is inherently too risky for a loan; (2) riskier borrowers are highly lucrative, as long as you charge a high enough interest rate; (3) you can pass off the risk to someone else.

Countrywide Financial dove headlong into the subprime swamp starting about 2003. So did the majority of the country's most established commercial banks, from Citigroup and Washington Mutual to Wachovia and National City. Wall Street's biggest and most prestigious firms were falling over themselves to get in on the action too. Not only were they buying up trillions of dollars in risky mortgages, but they were buying the mortgage companies themselves in an effort to control the entire financial chain.

In less than five years, subprime lending had expanded from

a fringe business to a central pillar of the mortgage industry. By 2006, subprime loan issues would top out at $600 billion—one out of every five new mortgages that year. Traditional lenders had little choice but to jump in and compete.

To my surprise, Michael Strauss wasn't anything like the Orange County wheeler-dealers. In fact, he had been a late and almost reluctant arrival on the double-black-diamond slopes of mortgage lending. As recently as 2003, one year before I became a customer, American Home had barely dabbled in exotic mortgages. Eighty percent of its loans had been the very definition of stodgy and safe: they "conformed" to the plain-vanilla requirements of Fannie Mae and Freddie Mac, the government-sponsored mortgage finance companies. Less than 3 percent of its mortgages had been classified as Alt-A, and even fewer had been subprime.

Strauss refused to talk to me for this book. In fact, he refused to acknowledge my existence. I didn't take it personally. By the time I tried to contact him in early 2008, he and other top executives at American Home were fending off a huge class-action lawsuit by shareholders. In bankruptcy court, meanwhile, creditors, home owners, and former employees were all pressing their claims on what remained of his company. The litigation was likely to last for years. Though Strauss stayed in touch with some of his former executives, he stayed out of sight as much as possible.

Former executives and employees of American Home describe a man who seemed like anything but a swashbuckling risk taker. Nearly six feet four inches tall and stocky, he was cerebral, analytical, and often remote. He had grown up and gone to college in the Midwest, and he had spent his career in New York City and Long Island. In a business based heavily on salesmanship and self-promotion, Strauss stayed out of the spotlight. He didn't star in his own TV commercials. He didn't give many interviews. He didn't even like being photographed by his own marketing department. "The two words I would use are 'frumpy' and 'boring,'" said Todd Hawkins, a former loan officer for American Home in Charlottesville, Virginia.

Strauss avoided attention as intently as many of his rivals clamored for it. When he did get up on a stage at a sales meeting, he tended to be plodding and dull. In his heart, Strauss was a numbers man who liked to bury himself in data about net interest margins, credit spreads, and hedging strategies. "Mike is friendly, but he has no charisma," said Kathleen Heck, a former executive vice president who had overseen the company's recruiting and training. "He left that to other people."

When Strauss did speak in public, he sounded more like a cautious accountant than an entrepreneur touting his vision. "We provide a balanced opportunity," he told CNBC in 2003, when his company's loan volumes had skyrocketed tenfold in the previous four years. Far from hyping his track record, Strauss cautiously predicted that 2004 would be "our second best year ever"—which turned out to be an understatement.

Starting in 2004, everything changed. Strauss didn't simply go with the flow. He changed his strategy on every front, and each change added to the risk he was taking on. He appeared to believe so ardently in the huge profits from high-risk lending that he wanted a piece of the action for himself. American Home abruptly shifted its focus to Alt-A and expanded its "wholesale" business; instead of making loans almost entirely through its own loan officers, it recruited thousands of independent brokers, who were harder to control. But Strauss's most important and fatal change was to multiply many times over his bet on American Home's riskiest mortgages.

Until 2004, American Home had been like thousands of other small mortgage companies: it had originated loans and then resold them as soon as the papers were signed. Usually, it had sold the loans to big banks and Wall Street firms. That was standard procedure for the new breed of "nonbank" lenders, who didn't have much capital of their own. A Wall Street firm like Bear Stearns or a big commercial bank like Citigroup would buy their loans at a healthy margin over their own costs. As the "loan originator," Strauss would pocket an up-front profit and the Wall Street firm would put the loans into a trust, which would get its money by selling complicated mortgage-backed bonds to investors. This was "securitization," and it spread the risk among all the investors. They would take the hit for any defaults and foreclosures, but there weren't many of those. For practical purposes, Strauss and all the other mortgage lenders were the marketing arms for Wall Street.

Strauss, however, seemed to believe his risky new loans would actually deliver the exaggerated returns they promised. He was so sure they would pay off, in fact, that he decided to start holding more and more of them at American Home. Starting in 2004, American Home Mortgage turned itself into a giant hedge fund— a "real estate investment trust," or REIT, which was technically like a partnership organized to manage a real estate investment portfolio. Instead of selling all its mortgages to Wall Street, it began holding billions of dollars' worth of them in order to reap the higher rates. Strauss's strategy was much riskier than simply exposing American Home to the potential losses from soured loans. Because American Home didn't have enough capital on its own to hold the mortgages—it was a marketing company, after all, not a bank—it borrowed 90–95 percent of the money to buy them.

The move was mystifying. I could understand that a hard-nosed, aggressive lender would be happy to make dubious loans if he knew someone else would take all the risk off his hands. If a schmuck newspaper reporter was clamoring to borrow more than he could afford, and Citigroup or Merrill Lynch was dying to put up the money, why get in the way? In fact, critics of the mortgage industry frequently accused the modern lenders of being reckless because they no longer had any "skin in the game," a stake of their own in making sure that the loans they made were solid.

Why, though, would a shrewd and cold-blooded insider get so excited that he had to invest in the dubious mortgages himself? The genius of modern capitalism, as Alan Greenspan would say, was that it could guide and regulate itself through the power of rational self-interest. People took risks, and they often made mistakes, but they also would use all the available information to discern what course of action was in their own self-interest.

Strauss, by contrast, appeared to believe his own marketing. He sometimes boasted about being "countercyclical," by which he meant departing from the industry's prevailing trends and being well positioned for a change in the marketplace. Yet he embraced the rush to riskier mortgages and the housing bubble, and his strategy assumed that the extraordinary conditions would keep going indefinitely. He had plenty of company. If I was like the Everyman for borrowers who ignored common sense in order to buy an overpriced house, Strauss was the Everyman for all the go-go lenders and Wall Street deal makers who ended up believing in the mania that they themselves had whipped up.

Strauss had not started out that way. Born and raised in Chicago, he had earned a bachelor's degree in business at Washington University in St. Louis and moved to New York in the early 1980s. He found work as a mortgage broker and ended up at the Wall Street firm of Kidder Peabody, which was then owned by General Electric. At the time, Kidder was one of the biggest traders and creators of mortgage-backed securities. The head of Kidder's mortgage department was Michael Vranos, who frequently boasted that he was paid as much as Jack Welch, GE's legendary chief executive.

I couldn't find out why Strauss quit Kidder in 1988 to enter the less glamorous business of mortgage lending. For the first five years, he was simply an independent mortgage broker, a person who earned commissions by lining up home buyers with lenders offering money. But by the early 1990s, Strauss had recruited a small force of loan officers around New York and evolved from being just a broker to being a small lender in his own right. In an interview with *Newsday* in 2003, he recounted how he had scraped together $250,000 and persuaded a bank to provide him with a $1 million line of credit. Using the credit line, he would finance a customer's mortgage, sell it to a bank or Wall Street firm, and repay his credit line. Then he would turn around and do it again.

In the jargon of the industry, American Home had become a "mortgage banker." It was a self-aggrandizing term, because there was nothing very banklike about a mortgage bank—no depositors, no tellers, no vaults, and almost no cash. It did mean that Strauss was more than just a sales agent. His company was actually financing loans.

Strauss got his first big break as a result of another bubble. In September 1999, less than a year before the dot-com bubble burst, he took American Home Mortgage public, in part by promoting its potential as an Internet-based mortgage lender. "We intend to expand our mortgage origination volume through the Internet and other more traditional changes," the company said in its prospectus that year. Touting its new subsidiary, MortgageSelect.com, American Home raised $15 million in an initial stock offering.

The Internet business never became a big part of the company, but Strauss benefited enormously from going public. Just a few months after American Home's shares started trading, Strauss quickly began using his stock as currency to finance a string of acquisitions around the country. In December 1999, American Home paid $7 million, most of it in newly issued shares, for Marina Mortgage, a lender in Irvine, California. That acquisition gave Strauss a crucial foothold in southern California. Over the next five years, American Home would buy up small lenders in Illinois, Pennsylvania, Maryland, and Indiana. In 2003, the company bought eighty-six branch offices from Washington Mutual, a huge bank on the West Coast that had become an aggressive player in both subprime and Alt-A mortgages.

Strauss had succeeded in stitching together a national organization. He persuaded many of the former owners of companies he had acquired to stay on, and he paid big sign-on bonuses to keep their loan officers. The company also invested in technology and back-office infrastructure to preapprove borrowers almost instantly, service customers, train salespeople, and launch new products.

"They were smart about how they did it, and they said all the right things," recalled Deborah Sturges, a former executive at Waterfield Financial in Fort Wayne, Indiana, which American Home bought in 2006. Strauss flew Waterfield's senior management to his offices on Long Island and had his top executives talk about their growth strategy and their skill in quickly matching new loans offered by competitors. "They said all the right things, about how we could build something much bigger because they had the resources," Sturges said. "I was a trusting midwesterner, and I bought it."

Strauss insisted to almost anyone who would listen that American Home had not become a subprime lender, because most of its borrowers still had high credit scores. To Strauss, credit scores were like a magic talisman that could reveal a borrower's soul in a single number. People with scores above 700 were people who had a long history of paying their bills on time. They were people who had shown they cared about their credit and could make sound decisions. "Our borrowers have a history of paying their obligations," he told investment analysts in a conference call in 2006. And it was true that, on average, American Home's borrowers continued to have credit scores above 700—solidly in "prime" territory.

But surrounded by cheap money and ferocious competitors, Strauss sharply lowered his standards. The first step was to greatly expand the range of high-wire loans for "prime" borrowers. It all seemed very scientific. American Home developed detailed rate sheets for dozens of unorthodox loan features. Every feature, or "risk factor," had its own price tag, in the form of an additional premium on top of a person's basic interest rate. The list included at least a half dozen low-doc loans. The tamest allowed borrowers to simply "state" their incomes but required them to document their assets and employment. Further down the list were the "no-ratio" loans, for which a borrower didn't even state an income but did document assets. At the bottom of the list were pure no-document loans, for which borrowers provided absolutely no financial information and the lender based everything on credit scores.

Loan officers could play with the automated underwriting system, mixing and matching features to test just how much risk the system would let a borrower get away with. If someone wanted to borrow $300,000 but earned only enough to qualify for $200,000, the loan officer could switch to a "stated-income loan" and let the customer state a higher number.

In another variation of "don't ask, don't tell," executives actively encouraged loan officers to switch between different kinds of loans. To protect the company from being accused of collaborating on a fraudulent mortgage, senior executives warned loan officers that they couldn't switch to a different loan after they had pushed the button and formally submitted an application for approval. "The LO can play around with the loan all they want to on Loan Soft as long as it has NOT been released to processing," wrote Melissa Johnson, an underwriting executive at company headquarters, in a memo to branch managers in 2006.

The shift toward riskier loans was apparent in American Home's annual report for 2004. The volume of Alt-A loans, which were mostly low-doc loans and loans with little or no down payment, totaled only $569 million in 2003, but that total quintupled to $3 billion—15 percent of total loans—in 2004. And that was just the start.

Wall Street firms' insatiable hunger for higher-yielding mortgages continued unabated, and rating agencies like Moody's and Standard & Poor's were giving triple-A ratings to securities backed only by true "subprime" mortgages. "It was like giving crack cocaine to the real estate industry," said Thomas Fiddler, a former executive vice president who oversaw much of American Home's lending in the Midwest. "If you didn't offer these products, you would effectively be rendered useless. Your salespeople would walk. The realtors would walk. Once the joker was out of the deck, you really had to play it."

Even as Strauss insisted that his customers were "high-credit-quality" borrowers, he rolled out a new series of "Choice" mortgages in early 2005 that were open even to people with disastrous credit. "Choice Platinum" offered home buyers 100 percent financing, "Full-Doc to No-Doc," at what the executives boasted were "A-paper rates." "Choice Flex" offered no-money-down financing to home buyers who had been in bankruptcy in the recent past. "Choice Investor XX" offered mortgages to people the moment they came out of bankruptcy.

"CHOICE FLEX IS HERE!" proclaimed Kenneth Hefner, a product support specialist in the Choice division, in an email to managers on May 27, 2005. "This program offers 100% financing down to a 580 FICO score (full document only), requires no BK seasoning [i.e., passage of time since a bankruptcy], disregards all mortgage lates less than 120 days and has minimal asset verification requirements."

Even the Choice loans, though, were like riding a bike with training wheels. Far more treacherous were the "Power ARMs," which American Home launched in early 2005. The Power ARMs were American Home's version of the "option ARM" or "pick-a-payment" mortgages. Option ARMs had been popularized by West Coast lenders like Washington Mutual and Golden States Financial, and they were arguably the worst mortgage ever invented. But because they allowed people to qualify for much bigger loans than had been remotely imaginable before, they had taken the country by storm. Even though they had barely existed in 2003, they accounted for 12 percent of all new mortgages in 2005.

Option ARMs were exquisitely designed to exploit the worst excesses of the housing bubble. They were perfect for fast-buck speculators, perfect for deceiving unsophisticated borrowers, and perfect for luring people with incomes into dream houses they could not possibly afford. At American Home, executives described option ARMs as "sophisticated tools" that enhanced a borrower's "flexibility." The basic idea seemed harmless enough: under a pay-option mortgage, borrowers had at least three different payment choices each month. They could pay the full principal and interest of a thirty-year loan; they could pay just the interest; or they could make an alluringly low "minimum payment."

The first two options were just camouflage for the real innovation: the minimum payment. As outlined in an internal marketing manual for loan officers, a person with a $562,500 mortgage could move in and pay only $1,559 a month the first year. By contrast, paying full principal and interest could easily cost at least $3,500 a month. "Keep your cash in your pocket, where you can use it for other things," an American Home brochure cheerily advised.

Power ARMs and other pay-option mortgages appealed to speculators who wanted to buy and resell houses for a fast profit within a few months. Condo and house flippers were making huge profits almost effortlessly in overheated markets like Las Vegas, Phoenix, and Palm Beach. Assuming that the price of a house or condo would climb by $20,000 over two or three months, as many of them were doing from 2004 until early 2006, the Power ARM offered incredible opportunities. A high-credit-quality borrower could get a Power ARM from American Home to finance 100 per-cent of the purchase price, escaping the need for a down payment. And the low monthly payments meant that the carrying cost was much lower than for any other kind of mortgage.

Senior executives at American Home said the company had no choice but to keep up with its rivals. "Wall Street thought they were OK," said one of Strauss's top lieutenants. "I didn't give it a second thought."

Yet it's hard to imagine a mortgage rigged with more booby traps and deceptions.

American Home—along with most of its rivals and thousands of smaller fly-by-night brokers—promoted the loan as offering a "1.25 percent starter rate." Borrowers would see "1.25 percent" on direct-mail flyers, on their initial loan estimates, and often on their final loan papers. That number was almost a complete fabrication. It had nothing to do with the interest rate a person was actually charged. At best, it referred to the interest rate a borrower would be charged for the first three months. After that, the real rate would be at least 5 percent and would adjust every month in line with one of the major indices of interbank lending rates.

The internal marketing manual made your head spin, but the rationale for calling it a "1.25 percent" loan came down to this: *if* you had an interest rate of only 1.25 percent on a loan of $562,500, *then* your monthly payment for principal and interest *would be* only $1,559. Of course, no one actually was saying your interest rate *was* 1.25 percent. Your real rate would be 5 percent or 7 percent or higher, and your real payment would be about $3,500 a month. But the $1,559 would be your "minimum payment," and your monthly bill would list that as the amount due for "principal and interest."

To be sure, the bottom section of American Home's monthly bill would remind you that you had other choices, but the first option was always the minimum payment. If you paid the minimum, American Home would add about $2,000 in "deferred interest" to your loan balance each month. If you kept that up for five years, your debt would have climbed by almost $100,000—plus the interest on the interest.

The internal marketing manual listed all kinds of people who could benefit from the "flexibility" of the Power ARM: newlywed borrowers, newly divorced borrowers, self-employed people, seasonally employed people, "trailing spouses." It even said the Power ARM was great for retired people. But the marketing brochures didn't even hint at what would happen when the "option" period ended after five years: if you had been paying only the minimum all along, you would face the mother of all payment shocks.

For starters, you would suddenly have to start making the full payments for interest and principal—in itself almost double the original minimum payment. On top of that, you would owe tens of thousands of dollars more than you had at the start. And as if that weren't enough, you would have to squeeze all those repayments into twenty-five years rather than thirty. Even if your interest rate wasn't higher—though it probably would be, because of how the formula was structured—the monthly payments could easily be almost triple the original minimum. And those payments wouldn't be optional. So much for keeping cash in your pocket.

Instead of helping loan officers explain all that to potential borrowers, American Home's manual described a new computer "worksheet" that would vividly highlight how much lower a person's monthly payments could be. The sample worksheet showed that the minimum monthly payment on a $225,000 mortgage would start out at only $749 and that the payment on a comparable thirty-year fixed-rate loan would be $1,330. Yet it offered no estimates of how much debt a person would accumulate or what would happen in year 6.

When American Home borrowed $5 billion in 2004 and transformed into a REIT to buy back about the same volume of its own mortgage-backed securities, Strauss boldly predicted that most of American Home's profits would soon come from its investment portfolio. But he also predicted that the investment portfolio would have a debt-to-equity ratio between 8 to 1 and 12 to 1.

Put another way, Strauss was borrowing about 90 percent of the purchase price of his mortgages and betting that the profit stream from those higher interest rates would more than offset the losses from defaults. If American Home bought back $1 billion worth of mortgages yielding an average interest rate of 7 percent, and borrowed 90 percent of the money at an interest rate of 5 percent, it would make a profit on the "spread" of 2 percentage points—$18 million. It would also earn the full 7 percent, or another $7 million, on its own investment of $100 million. The bottom line: American

Home would be making an annual return of $25 million, or 25 percent, on its investment of $100 million. At a time of low interest rates and cutthroat competition, that was a spectacular return.

American Home was simply one small example of Wall Street's broader infatuation with "leverage," or using borrowed money to torque up returns on seemingly safe investments. In April 2004, at the same time that Strauss was shifting gears, Wall Street's five biggest investment banks persuaded the supine Securities and Exchange Commission to relax a long-standing regulation that limited the amount of debt their brokerage units could take on. Henry M. Paulson Jr., then chairman of Goldman Sachs and soon to become treasury secretary under President Bush, was among those who led the charge. As reported by Stephen Labaton in *The New York Times*, the SEC's rule change immediately freed up billions of dollars in reserves at Goldman, Morgan Stanley, Merrill Lynch, Bear Stearns, and Lehman Brothers. The debt ratios at most of those companies shot up to more than 30 to 1, meaning that they had at least $30 in debt for every $1 in equity. Much of that leverage went into mortgage-backed securities, and some of it undoubtedly ended up financing part of American Home's leveraged portfolio of high-risk mortgages.

But just like the condo flippers in Vegas who were using as little of their own money as possible to buy and resell properties, the whole strategy assumed that home prices would keep climbing, at least at a modest pace. It also assumed that people would pay their mortgages as reliably as they had in the past. The problem was that people were no longer buying homes as they had in the past. People were looking at houses not as homes but as investments. And a lot of people were looking at them as highly speculative investments that would earn them a profit almost overnight.

Meanwhile, Strauss was quietly taking on even more risk than seemed apparent at the time. Not only was he betting on the come about his mortgages; he was actually placing a big part of his bet on his most exotic and least-tested product of all—the Power ARMs.

In a conference call with Wall Street analysts in October 2005, Strauss was asked about $1.3 billion worth of mortgages that American Home had put into its portfolio in the previous three months. The move had raised eyebrows because American Home had not bothered to securitize these mortgages and hold them as mortgage-backed bonds. Bonds were much easier to trade than the underlying mortgages, and they were supposed to reduce risk by containing a diversified pool of loans from around the country.

Strauss acknowledged that most of the $1.3 billion in raw mortgages was in fact in option ARMs, and he acknowledged that some of them were for 100 percent of the value of the property. That meant some of the borrowers had none of their own money in the deal. "A large portion was option ARMs," Strauss said. "We think that that is an attractive product, because it offers a high yield, it reprices continuously, it has a slow life—the life is lengthened by prepayment penalties—and we think we have successfully taken the credit risk off the table by buying supplemental insurance."

To most people, it sounded like gobbledygook. If you deconstructed the jargon, however, you could hear Strauss expressing the core principles of go-go lending. In referring to "high yield," he was pointing out that risky borrowers bring higher profits. By saying it "reprices continuously," he meant that the interest rate adjusted with the market monthly from day one and that American Home would earn higher returns on the loans. And by referring to "supplemental insurance," he was saying he could lay the risk off on someone else.

By the end of 2005, Strauss had more than doubled the size of his portfolio, to $14 billion, and the portfolio was racking up eye-popping returns. On a conference call with analysts, Strauss said that the portfolio was earning a 25 percent return on equity and that percentage would probably get even higher. "As I have indicated, the return to equity from loans held for investment carried on a cost basis is projected to exceed 25 percent annually," he told them.

Strauss was so confident, in fact, that he was actually borrowing an even higher percentage of the money than before. Instead of borrowing $8 or $12 for every $1 American Home was investing of its own money in its portfolio, as Strauss had originally planned, American Home was talking about going as high as 18 to 1. Now *that* was gangsta.

4

MAGICAL THINKING, REAL DEBTS

The icy slap of reality hit me two weeks after New Year's Day in January 2005. I walked out of the *Times'* Washington bureau, two blocks north of the White House, and crossed Farragut Square to my bank. I had a bad feeling about what the ATM would reveal about my balance, but I was shocked when I looked at the receipt: $196. For practical purposes, we were broke.

It seemed impossible. After buying the house in August, we had still had a cash cushion of $12,000 from selling my shares of company stock. I had known the cushion wouldn't last forever, and we had faced some big start-up costs. We had had to ship Patty's furniture to Washington, pay airfare for her and the children, and buy things for the house. On top of that, Patty had had to navigate an unfamiliar job market and hadn't started earning money until after Labor Day. And then there was Christmas, I remembered with a

Grinch-like groan. To celebrate our first Christmas together, we had bought Apple iPods for the boys—$1,500. But $12,000 in less than six months? Above and beyond our regular income? That was a very fast burn rate.

What were we going to burn now—now that the spare cash was gone?

My stomach churning, I reached Patty on her cell phone as she was running errands. "We are out of money," I snapped, skipping over any warm-up chat. I was scared and angry, partly at her, even though our predicament was my fault as much as anybody's.

"What do you mean, we're out of money?" she asked in bewilderment.

"I mean, I just checked my bank account, and we are out of money," I repeated, my voice rising in panic. "We can't buy anything!"

My next paycheck would come in about a day or so, but that was entirely reserved for the February mortgage payment. We didn't have enough cash to cover more than a week's worth of groceries and gasoline.

"How the hell could we have run through so much money so quickly?" I asked her accusingly.

Patty wasn't sharing my shock. "I don't know what's going on," she responded, sounding hurried. "Let's talk about it when you get home."

I didn't have a better suggestion, but my temper was rising and I gave voice to my inner dictator. "OK," I said. "Just don't spend anything. We have to stop spending money right now—no spending at all."

Patty knew I was bringing home less money than most cab drivers. But we had both assumed she could earn enough for us to get by. We didn't have any idea how she would do it; we were both simply sure that she could do it.

She had spent the two prior decades as a stay-at-home mother in Los Angeles. And although she had helped organize a local pre-school and had almost completed the requirements for a master's degree in Latin American studies at UCLA, her last official job had been back in the early 1980s. She had been an editor at a politi-cal polling company when she and her then-husband were living in Washington DC. Patty had completed a graduate program in publishing at George Washington University, and she hadn't lost her chops as both a meticulous proofreader and a line editor who could make uninspired writing sound elegant. That said, her days as a professional editor had stopped before anybody was using computers.

She felt intimidated looking for new work, and she doubted that her skills were worth any real money. After more than twenty years as a self-confident, stay-at-home mother, the pressure to go job hunting had made her anxious and intimidated for the first time in her life. She felt as if she were asking for charity every time she went into a job interview. And although she understood that peo-ple had to market themselves, she detested the idea of pretending to be self-assured and ambitious. She felt as green as an eighteen-year-old.

Not surprisingly, Patty's reentry into the job market was bumpy. She found work as a freelance editor, signing up with a temp agency that specialized in editorial services. But although the pay was fairly good, at $30 an hour, the volume of work didn't come close to equaling a full-time job. So when Saks Fifth Avenue offered her a full-time job selling high-end clothing on commission—something she knew about and loved—she grabbed it. But that turned out to be just as grim, with her take-home income averaging only about $2,400 a month—not enough to cover our bills when my take-home pay was going straight to the mortgage.

Patty's small weekly paychecks kept us going on daily expenses. In mid-February of 2005, I got an extra $5,000 from the *Times* for all the extra days I had worked in the previous six months. In April, we got a tax refund of almost $4,000.

Those occasional windfalls, though, couldn't fix our basic shortfall: we were spending way more than we were earning. Our income was less than we had assumed, and our spending was more than we had assumed. In the euphoria of moving in together, we had both succumbed to magical thinking—about ourselves, as well as money. The ATM shock had been the first of many early warnings, but I quickly learned that you can spend more than you earn for a long time before you can no longer put food on the table.

I had assumed that we could squeak by if Patty brought home a net income of about $2,500 a month to supplement the meager $2,777 of my own paycheck that remained after payments to my ex-wife. Patty had assumed that she could easily earn that much money, which translated to a gross income of $40,000 a year.

Unfortunately, my magical fantasy was that Patty would become, well, an ambitious go-getter. "This can really be an exciting new chapter of your life," I kept telling her. She would start out by impressing people with her skills as an editor, I would say, and then she'd schmooze her way into more lucrative opportunities. Who knew what possibilities would open up for her? It didn't occur to me that she might not want to start that new chapter, or might not be able to. Nor did it occur to me that I wouldn't have fallen in love with her if she *had* been a career-climbing opportunist. The last person I wanted to marry was someone who adored job pressure, brought work home at night, and was glued to a Blackberry.

Patty had a very different dream. "I feel as if I am finally at home," she had exclaimed as soon as we moved into the house. She meant it literally, because she had lived in Washington years earlier and felt more at home there than in Los Angeles. She also seemed to mean that she was returning to something like her former life. She could settle down and do the things she had always been best at: making a new home, nurturing her children, and loving me. The money, she figured, would take care of itself.

After weighing her job options, Patty decided to work at Saks. She liked fashion and knew that experienced salespeople at Saks often earned more than $50,000 a year. The hours were also good—10:00 a.m. to 6:00 p.m.—but her take-home income barely hit $2,500 a month during the peak holiday rush. By the spring, she felt she was trapped in a low-paying job, so she quit to try her hand once again as a freelance editor.

Then there was Patty's ex-husband. Patty and I had blithely assumed that he would make his $700 monthly payment just because a judge had ordered him to. But this assumption ignored an obvious problem: Patty's ex-husband had been behind on his child support payments almost the entire time they had been separated, and he showed no evidence of changing his ways. Within months of her arrival in Washington, he had already fallen thousands of dollars behind. We were infuriated. But really, what had we expected?

Tensions were building and we weren't even married yet. I was anxious and often angry about money. Patty felt guilt-ridden and defensive. Neither of us thought the other understood the reality of our situation.

We had very different ideas about money. Patty spent little on herself, but she spent freely on whatever she thought was necessary for the family. She refused to scrimp on top-quality produce, Starbucks coffee, bottled juices, fresh cheeses, and clothing for the children and for me. She regularly bought me new shirts and ties to replace the frayed and drab ones in my closet. To Patty, some things you simply had to buy. She thought it wasn't worth agonizing over nickels and dimes. I was almost exactly the opposite. My answer to any money problem was to stop spending. I would skip lunch at work to save $7. If I arrived at the subway just before the end of rush hour, I would wait for five minutes to save fifty cents on the fare. If Patty had not insisted on a home subscription to *The New York Times,* I would have contented myself with reading it online and picking up a free copy at the office.

We were both building up grudges. "You can't keep second-guessing me," she told me angrily. "It's small-minded and petty, and it's not very attractive." But I was beginning to wonder whether she had any clue about how money worked. We were lurching from paycheck to paycheck, one big car repair or home repair away from disaster.

The gulf between us surfaced when we sat down with a minister to talk about marriage plans. Betsy Hague had started her career as a Catholic nun but had left the church to get married and become an Episcopalian minister. Now in her seventies, Hague had agreed to marry us, but she insisted that we answer a detailed questionnaire aimed at measuring our compatibility.

"You have some big differences that you really need to talk through," she informed us somberly as we reviewed the results with her. Patty and I had either disagreed with each other or been equally uncertain on 90 percent of our answers. We had given different answers to every financial question except one, and the one we agreed on was hardly reassuring: we both thought our finances after getting married would be bad. "You don't agree on anything about financial management, and that's the most pressing problem you face," Hague told us, looking worried. Despite her unease, she agreed to marry us as long as we sat down with her to work through some of our issues.

Meanwhile, neither of us was paying attention to how catastrophically easy our bank had made it to build up debt. The key was the overdraft protection—more accurately described as "bounced-check loans." Every time I overdrew my checking account by even a few dollars, the bank would tap my MasterCard for $100, helpfully deposit the cash in my account, and charge me $10 for the privilege.

Over the months that we still had our initial cash cushion, we had stayed out of trouble. But once the last of it evaporated in January, Patty and I began unwittingly tapping into our credit line at a terrifying pace. Five dollars overdrawn because of school supplies for Emily? $100 from the MasterCard. Fifteen bucks over because of gasoline? $100 from the MasterCard. $305 because you were temporarily out of cash for groceries? No problem! Uncle MasterCard would front us $400.

"What's this?" I hollered one Sunday as I was paying the bills. "We owe $1,900 on the SunTrust MasterCard." Patty glared at me. "You insist on having your paychecks and your expense reimbursements go into a separate account," she said. "I have no way of knowing what's going on with our money."

At her insistence, I grimly reviewed the list of purchases. Groceries, gasoline, the copayment for a doctor's visit, phone bill, more groceries and gasoline, clothes for Emily and Will. Nothing seemed superfluous, but it added up to more money than we had.

Our debt spiraled up faster than I had ever dreamed possible. Chase Bank had cold-called me to offer a "platinum" card with no interest charges for the first six months. I took them up on it and shifted $3,000 in debt from my old card onto the new

Chase card. But instead of paying down the balance before the interest charges began, I let it balloon to $6,000. Chase had sent us blank checks that we could use to either pay bills or give ourselves cash advances. I dismissed them as a cheap trick to lure dimwits into borrowing more money. By March, I decided I needed a cheap trick. Swallowing my pride, I grabbed one of the checks and used it to pay down $1,000 on my more expensive credit card.

By May 2005, the balances on our two main credit cards had surged to $9,000, and one of them was charging us 18 percent interest. Every day I felt as if my head were spinning and my stomach had butterflies. Patty was frightened of me. She dreaded every time I sat down to pay the bills, waiting for me to panic and lose my temper.

"I have a plan," I said bravely one day. I was reprising the knight in *Monty Python and the Holy Grail,* who tells King Arthur to sneak into the French fortress by building a giant Trojan rabbit—but then forgets to tell anybody to hide inside the rabbit. My plan wasn't as funny, but it was just as contorted: I would borrow enough cash from my 401(k) retirement account to pay off the credit cards and keep enough cash to . . . pay myself back. On May 6, I called up Vanguard, the mutual-fund company that managed my 401(k). "I need to take a loan against my account," I said.

Because 401(k) contributions offer big tax incentives to save for retirement, they are difficult to raid for quick cash—just as I would have done in a heartbeat if I had been allowed. Except for a short list of approved emergencies, such as an imminent foreclosure on your house—people under the age of fifty-five are not allowed to permanently withdraw money. The rules did allow me to borrow money from my account, but I had to pay myself back every month through automated payroll withholdings. The loan had to be paid off within seven years, with interest, so the monthly withholdings could take a real bite.

"What would my payments be if I took out $15,000?" I asked. The customer service rep estimated they would be about $325 a month. But, he added helpfully, I was allowed to borrow as much as $19,000. That would mean repayments of $382 a month for seven years. I felt trapped. What was worse—losing $382 a month out of my already meager paycheck, or running out of cash again? Then I hit on a delirious brainstorm: I would take the larger sum, keep some of the extra cash for emergencies, but also use some of it to offset the withholdings from my paycheck.

The sheer nuttiness of this didn't register at the time. I was borrowing money from myself in order to pay off debts, but I planned to borrow more than I needed in order to help pay myself back.

Why not?

5

ALAN GREENSPAN

Alan Greenspan sounded like a shaken and humbled old man. Nearly three years after he had stepped down as Fed chairman, he was once again testifying before a House committee. It was October 2008. Banks and Wall Street firms were failing, the economy was in a free fall, and the Bush Treasury Department was lurching from one gigantic bailout to another. For decades, Greenspan had championed free markets and self-interest. Now, he admitted, he had put too much faith in the self-correcting power of free markets and not enough in the self-destructive power of markets gone amok. "Those of us who have looked to the self-interest of lending institutions to protect shareholders' equity, myself included, are in a state of shocked disbelief," he told the House Committee on Oversight and Government Reform.

He had been stunned by the debacle over subprime lending and sickened by Wall Street's role in promoting bad loans. The exotic financial instruments that had been invented to reduce risk had instead nearly wrecked the financial system. "This modern risk-management paradigm held sway for decades," he said. "The whole intellectual edifice, however, collapsed in the summer of last year."

Watching Greenspan, I didn't know whether I felt sadness or out-rage. Only three years earlier, as he had been preparing to step down after eighteen years as chairman of the Federal Reserve, economists had hailed him as probably the best central banker in history. Now he was under fire from Democratic and Republican lawmakers alike, who wanted him to admit he had been wrong and who interrupted him almost every time he tried to defend and explain himself. But when it came to assigning responsibility for the biggest financial catastrophe in almost a century, many roads led to Greenspan.

———————————

When I first met Greenspan in early 2003, he immediately struck me as one of the most intriguing public figures I had ever encoun-tered. Of all the people with outsized reputations I had met in Wash-ington, Alan Greenspan was one of the very few who impressed me as even more larger-than-life up close than he did in public. When he sat down for an off-the-record conversation, he talked as if the world was a giant Rubik's Cube. He seemed to delight in turning questions over and over in his mind. Even though he had the face of an aging basset hound and his hair had become wispy thin, he seemed fresher and more inquisitive than most people half his age. If you asked him a question that intrigued him, his face would light up and he would dive into a rumination about the possible answers.

It was a relief to talk with Greenspan after trying to listen to senior officials in the Bush administration. Bush people were the Stepford wives of government. With few exceptions, they always talked as if they were reading from scripts and ignored questions they didn't want to discuss. They weren't just secretive; they were boring. At least Greenspan was interesting.

But the maestro had blind spots, and they contributed mightily to the housing and mortgage fiasco. He firmly believed real estate was a local business, and he acknowledged that it often suffered from local bubbles and busts, but a nationwide bubble that could derail the whole economy? "Very unlikely."

It wasn't just an economic judgment. Greenspan thought the social and political benefits of home ownership were so powerful that it was hard to imagine a downside. He was convinced that being a home owner tied you more closely to the community. It made people better citizens and perhaps even better people, and ultimately made the country better and more stable. It was the same line as Karl Rove's, without the overt political overtones.

Greenspan also believed so strongly in the wisdom of free markets that he was loath to let the government ever intervene. If adults wanted to conduct transactions with each other, he believed, the government should not get in the way. A booming marketplace was almost by definition a good marketplace.

He especially adored all the new financial instruments and technologies that made it easier to disperse risk. Whether they were futures that allowed you to bet on the next change in interest rates or credit-default swaps to protect you from bond defaults, they generally made financial markets safer, smoother, and more stable. But as he later admitted, many of those instruments magnified the risk by aggravating the euphoria of the bubble and increasing speculative game-playing.

I was waiting in an ornate conference room near the chairman's office when Greenspan quietly walked in. He moved a bit stiffly and shook my hand without saying much. It was early 2003, and the *Times* had recently assigned me to cover the Federal Reserve. Greenspan had known hundreds of reporters over the years, and he often sat down with them for off-the-record conversations. It wasn't a model of transparency, but it helped us understand his often delphic statements in public.

I had no idea what to ask. I couldn't think of a probing question about the economy either, so I decided to punt. "Could you describe some of the economic models that guide your thinking about the economy?" I asked. It sounded like a sophisticated way of asking, "Alan, what do you do on the 350 days a year when you are *not* meeting to set interest rates?"

Ever so politely, Greenspan said he didn't much care for models. What really interested him, he said, were "anomalies"—developments that seemed to contradict the models. The best clues to what was really happening, he continued, were things that you didn't expect to see, things that forced you to take a fresh look at your assumptions.

It was a jewel of an insight, and it was part of what made Greenspan great. Most economists liked to identify rules to help forecast the economy, but Greenspan liked exceptions to the rules. It wasn't that he ignored the standard models any more than he ignored conventional wisdom. He simply saw them as the starting point, rather than the final word. He looked at familiar data with fresh eyes, raising questions that others didn't think to ask and then digging deep into more obscure data to find the answers.

"There's a certain really quite unimaginable intellectual interest that one gets," he told reporters after President George W. Bush announced plans to nominate him for a fifth term as Fed chairman. "It's like eating peanuts. You keep doing it, keep doing it; and you never get tired because the future is always ultimately unknowable."

Greenspan's eye for anomalies led to his greatest triumph as Fed chairman. Starting in the mid-1990s, he became increasingly convinced that American productivity—the amount produced per hour of work—was climbing faster than the official data indicated. If he was right, the implications were momentous.

The standard economic models assumed that the Fed had to impose a speed limit on the economy based on its underlying "potential" for growth. Economists based this speed limit on what they call the "natural rate of unemployment" or the so-called Non-Accelerating Inflation Rate of Unemployment (NAIRU, to devotees). If unemployment fell below the "natural rate," employers would have to raise wages faster than productivity and inflation would pick up. At that point, the Fed would have to hit the brakes by raising interest rates. However, if productivity suddenly started climbing faster, the Fed could wait longer. If productivity were higher than previously thought, the higher output per hour would offset the cost of higher wages.

Greenspan's suspicions stemmed partly from the fact that the official numbers didn't add up. Corporate profit margins were as wide as ever, even though real wages were rising and consumer prices were stable. It seemed impossible for all three things to be happening at once—unless productivity had accelerated. Many of his colleagues were deeply skeptical about the theory and unconvinced by the evidence. By 1996, several members of the Federal Open Market Committee—the all-important group that sets interest rates—were pushing to start raising rates immediately.

Greenspan dug in and eventually convinced the skeptics to hold off on a rate increase and see what happened. The rest was history: the United States enjoyed a golden period of low inflation, blazing job growth, and rising wealth at all income levels. The chairman had been right. "It was the most brilliant forecasting call I can think of in my entire career as a professional economist," said Laurence H. Meyer, a Fed governor at the time who called himself a "grudging" convert to Greenspan's views.

Greenspan didn't fit into any kind of neat box or category. He had studied music before he studied economics, and he had played jazz saxophone in Henry Jerome's dance band. As a young adult, he had been a disciple of Ayn Rand and her philosophy of "rational self-interest," but he never seemed comfortable with dogma and disavowed some of his early Randian ideas. Although he was a life-long Republican, he was hardly a party loyalist. As Fed chairman, he incurred the wrath of President George H. W. Bush for not cutting rates fast enough in the early 1990s. By contrast, Greenspan got along brilliantly with Democrats like Bill Clinton and Robert E. Rubin.

In Greenspan's mind, the world was raucous and unpredictable but also vibrant and dynamic. He embraced Joseph Schumpeter's view of capitalism as "creative destruction." Although he acknowledged that capitalism required laws and courts to resolve conflicts fairly, he also believed that a dynamic economy wasn't possible if people didn't have the freedom to take risks and make mistakes. Bouts of euphoria and panic were a natural part of the process.

Greenspan also knew how difficult it was to distinguish speculative mania from a boom fueled by fundamental change. He had been the one, after all, who had spooked markets in 1996 by publicly musing whether surging stock prices that year stemmed from "irrational exuberance." As it happened, the stock market was still in the early phase of its epic boom that lasted almost five more years.

After the technology stock bubble finally burst in 2000, Greenspan staunchly argued that the Fed would have caused more harm than good if it had tried to puncture the bubble in advance. The better strategy, he argued, was to wait and clean up the mess afterward. "We recognized that, despite our suspicions, it was very difficult to definitively identify a bubble until after the fact—that is, when its bursting confirmed its existence," Greenspan declared in August 2002, at a Fed symposium in Jackson Hole, Wyoming.

His deeper argument was more Zen-like: increased volatility went hand in hand with greater economic stability. He had often marveled that the dot-com implosion, which led to $6 *trillion* in losses, had not caused the collapse of a single major financial institution. Indeed, he suggested that the same changes that had fueled the bubble—technological advances, increased competition, deregulation—had also made the economy more adaptable and resilient. "We resurrected the dynamism of previous generations of Americans," he told the elite group assembled in Jackson Hole. "Somewhat surprisingly," he continued, the result was "an apparent reduction in the volatility of output."

No matter where he started, Greenspan seemed to end up at the same place: interfering with how people pursued their rational self-interest was a losing proposition and would cause more trouble than it prevented.

At the same time, Greenspan did not trust his laissez-faire instincts so much that he was ready to leave the economy's fate in the hands of random market forces. After the stock market collapsed in 2000 and the economy started to slide toward recession, he fought back with the full force of the Federal Reserve.

Starting in January 2001, the Fed opened the spigots of cheap money by lowering interest rates to rock bottom. By August, policy makers had cut the benchmark federal funds rate—the rate that banks charge each other on overnight loans of their reserves—by almost half, to 3.5 percent from 6.5 percent. After the terrorist attacks on September 11, they cut the rate in half again; and eventually they lowered it to just 1 percent in 2003. Interest rates on mortgages didn't fall quite as sharply as that, but they, too, dropped to levels most people weren't old enough to remember. The rate on a thirty-year fixed-rate mortgage sank from about 8.5 percent in May 2000 to about 5.2 percent in June 2003.

To home owners, home buyers, and the housing industry, this was money from heaven. If you hadn't lost your job, you could pay almost one-third more for a house in 2003 as in 2001, yet the monthly payment would not be any higher on the more expensive purchase. Alternatively, a family could refinance its $200,000 house, borrowing an extra $80,000 against the equity in the home, and its monthly payment for principal and interest would remain unchanged at about $1,537. Even though the United States was in a recession for much of 2001, home sales, home building, and home prices all shot up even faster than they had since the start of the boom around 1995.

None of this was an accident. Fed officials consciously pinned their hopes for an economic recovery at least partly on the housing sector. They didn't have much choice. With technology companies decimated by the collapse of their stock prices and businesses scaling back after massive outlays for new equipment and software, business investment was utterly stagnant. Making matters worse, manufacturers were being hammered. Not only were they swamped by surging imports from China and other countries, but the relatively high value of the dollar made their products expensive in foreign markets. Housing, it appeared, was the only game in town.

"Facilitating an increase in residential construction puts resources to use that would otherwise lie idle," said Donald Kohn, a highly respected Fed governor with close ties to Greenspan, in 2003. Kohn admitted that housing prices had "skyrocketed," but he meticulously described how most of the other areas of growth had been shut down for the time being.

Greenspan had been keenly aware for years that the housing market was important for much more than new construction jobs. As Greg Ip of the *Wall Street Journal* reported in 2003, Greenspan had noticed as far back as the 1960s that housing wealth was a potentially important source of consumer spending power. Whether by spending some of the profits they reaped from selling their homes or by borrowing more against their homes, people were turning some of their housing wealth into cash. It was a tiny phenomenon back then, but Greenspan argued that it could become a powerful force. By the late 1970s, he had presented his own evidence that capital gains from housing had a bigger impact on consumer spending than did gains from families' stock portfolios. After becoming Fed chairman in 1987, he asked analysts to build databases to track the money people were pulling out of their houses. By 2000, millions of families were using their houses like ATM machines.

As he fought to revive the economy, Greenspan was elated that the Fed's rate cuts had prompted a tidal wave of new borrowing. "Last year was one of the most memorable years ever experienced by the home mortgage market," he exulted in a speech to community bankers in 2003. Home owners had refinanced about $1.7 trillion in mortgages the year before, he proudly reported, and had tapped their home equity for more than $300 billion in cash.

The obvious potential problem was that American families were racking up debt at a feverish pace. Adjusted for inflation, the average family's debt, including mortgages, climbed from $54,000 in 1990 to more than $80,000 in 2004. Mortgage foreclosures, credit card delinquencies, and personal bankruptcies were heading toward record levels.

"The fear I have is that the world is leveraged on low-interest borrowing," Allen Sinai, chief executive of Decision Economics, told me in March 2004. "It's like a drug, and you get hooked on it." What would happen when the Federal Reserve decided to crank interest rates back up to more normal levels, in order to prevent inflation from taking off again?

In a weird way, especially for a hard-nosed central banker, Greenspan seemed to like debt. In October 2004, when the household savings rate was flirting with zero and occasionally turning negative, Greenspan argued that rising debt was a sign of rising affluence. "For at least a half century, household debt has been rising faster than income, as ever-higher levels of discretionary income have increased the proportion of income spent on assets partially financed with debt." In fact, he had cobbled together a broad theory to argue that rising debt levels were natural not just for American consumers but for the United States as a whole.

The United States had become far and away the world's biggest debtor nation. It spent as much as $800 billion a year more than it produced, and it made up the shortfall by borrowing billions of dollars a day from other countries, notably China. Legions of economists warned that Americans would eventually regret the borrowing binge. Paul Volcker, Greenspan's predecessor as Fed chairman, predicted at one point that the odds of a bruising and "disorderly" correction in the currency markets were about 75 percent.

Greenspan thought such fears were overdone. Financial markets had become more global, meaning that the United States could tap into deeper pools of capital without feeling uncomfortably constrained by higher interest rates. Greenspan didn't deny that the United States faced some sort of limit on its borrowing, but he argued that the limits had become much wider and perhaps unknowable. In any case, it wasn't something he lost much sleep over.

Ben Bernanke, a Fed governor at the time who later succeeded Greenspan as chairman, proposed an even more convenient explanation: a "global savings glut" of extra money that needed a place to go. If there was a problem, Bernanke argued, it wasn't that Americans were borrowing too much. It was that countries like China and Japan didn't have enough investment opportunities at home for all their cash.

Greenspan liked Bernanke's idea so much that he immediately embraced it. He was even sunnier about the rising debt of American families. Far from being a sign of distress, he said, rising debt sometimes simply reflected rising family incomes. Families that had more discretionary income could afford to buy more big-ticket items that they paid off over time.

It was a strange argument: the more money you made, the more you would want to borrow. The problem was that median family incomes, after adjusting for inflation, had been either stagnant or declining for all but a handful of years since the 1970s. The main exception had been from 1995 to 2000, when people at all income levels made gains. But after the downturn of 2001, middle- and lower-income families had barely regained the ground they had lost. "To be sure, some households are stretched to the limits," Greenspan admitted in 2004, adding that the "persistently elevated bankruptcy rate remains a concern." But overall, he asserted, American households were in "reasonably good shape."

Greenspan was equally sanguine about subprime mortgages, which he viewed as making access to credit more democratic. "Innovation has brought about a multitude of new products, such as subprime loans and niche credit programs for immigrants," he said at a consumer affairs conference at the Fed in early 2005. "Where once more-marginal applicants would simply have been denied credit, lenders are now able to quite efficiently judge the risk posed by individual applicants and to price that risk appropriately."

It all made exquisite sense to a man who had once found epiphanies in the "objectivism" of Ayn Rand. Thanks to advances in credit scoring and computer modeling, it was easier to quantify a person's risk. The more you could quantify a risk, the more you could put a rational price on it and sell it. And if you could lower the risk by spreading it around to other investors, you could lower the price even more. Greenspan also believed that even the excesses of cowboy lending served the higher ideological goal of the ownership society.

"I was aware that the loosening of mortgage credit terms for subprime borrowers increased financial risk," Greenspan later recounted in his memoir, *The Age of Turbulence*. "But I believed then, as now, that the benefits of broadened home ownership are worth the risk. Protection of property rights, so critical to a market economy, requires a critical mass of owners to sustain political support." This was a rare hint of Greenspan's less-than-rational ideological side. In some ways, he was only reiterating Ronald Reagan's immortal remark that "nobody ever washed a rented car." Yet it was remarkable that a man whose economic insights were so penetrating allowed his political and cultural sympathies to blur his judgment in this case.

John C. Gamboa and Robert L. Gnaizda of the Greenlining Institute, a community group in San Francisco, visited Greenspan in 2004 and described a litany of deceptive practices that had trapped unsuspecting subprime home buyers. In many cases, Gamboa and Gnaizda told Greenspan, mortgage lenders and brokers had steered unsuspecting customers who qualified for traditional mortgages into far more expensive subprime loans.

"We knew he wouldn't agree to new regulations, so we tried to appeal to his free-market instincts," recalled Gnaizda, chief counsel for the Greenlining Institute. Instead of asking the Fed to support new regulations, they asked Greenspan to support a voluntary code of conduct for mortgage lenders. An outside organization would verify that a lender was following the code and provide its seal of approval. Greenspan expressed sympathy. He even added ruefully that some of the exotic new mortgages were so complicated that a person with a PhD in mathematics wouldn't understand them. Still, he declined to push for better practices. "He never gave us a good reason, but he didn't want to do it. He just wasn't interested," said Gnaizda.

The Fed chairman was hardly alone. Almost all the top bank regulators in the Bush administration vociferously praised "financial innovation" and sought to make life easy for the institutions they supervised. Except for the Fed, federal banking regulators received their funding from fees paid by the institutions they regulated, and agencies routinely competed with each other for dues-paying "members."

The Office of Thrift Supervision (OTS), which regulates the nation's thrift institutions, boasted for years on its Internet home page about the streamlined regulation it offered. In 2005, the OTS codified gaping loopholes in its stern admonishments against unsafe lending practices. In updating its examination manual, the agency warned that "no-document" liar's loans were "unsafe and unsound." But it gave lenders a green light if they immediately sold the loans to outside investors. Since that was the standard practice, the exception became the rule.

The agency gutted a similar warning against qualifying people for loans they couldn't realistically repay. It seemed like the first commandment of lending: people should be able to show they can afford the loan. Yet Wall Street banks cast that principle aside when they pushed lenders to crank up their volumes with no-doc and low-doc loans.

The OTS regulators sought to accommodate. In the 2005 examiners' manual, the agency warned thrifts not to qualify people only on the basis of their ability to pay the low initial "teaser rate." "Using the deep teaser rate to qualify a borrower can cause some home owners to qualify for mortgages that they would not qualify for under normal circumstances," the manual noted primly. But once again, it offered a "possible exception" for thrifts that immediately sold their loans to outside investors.

Greenspan was not in charge of the Office of Thrift Supervision or its sister agencies, the Office of the Comptroller of the Currency and the Federal Deposit Insurance Corporation. That said, the Federal Reserve worked directly with the other federal banking regulators to make changes in broad regulatory policies on lending, and the agencies usually announced those changes jointly. The Fed towered over all the other regulators in its political influence and credibility. Beyond that, Greenspan had so much personal authority that he could put tremendous pressure on Congress and on the other agencies simply by expressing his opinions in public.

"The Federal Reserve could have stopped this problem dead in its tracks," said Martin Eakes, chief executive of the Center for Responsible Lending, a nonprofit group in North Carolina that had exhaustively studied lending practices and raised alarms years earlier. "If the Fed had done its job, we would not have had the abusive lending and we would not have a foreclosure crisis in virtually every community across America."

Within the Fed, at least one person had been warning for years that the spiraling rise of subprime loans posed dangers. That person was Edward M. Gramlich, a Fed governor who had been appointed by President Clinton and spent much of his career analyzing issues tied to poverty. Gramlich, who died of cancer in 2007, was a gentle and cerebral economist in a city dominated by egotism. As head of the Fed's consumer affairs committee, a post that other Fed governors considered a backwater, Gramlich had spent years listening to both community groups and industry executives.

Gramlich had fought for years for rules to protect low-income home buyers from deceptive or predatory lending practices, as well as from practices that appeared to discriminate against blacks and ethnic minorities. The catchall phrase for discriminating against borrowers from racial or ethnic minorities was *redlining,* a term that referred to the practice of banks in earlier decades to draw real or metaphorical lines on maps around neighborhoods in which the banks did not want to make consumer or business loans. Community advocates and civil rights groups had long complained that redlining was simply a form of racial and ethnic discrimination.

By the late 1990s, the rise of subprime lending meant that fewer and fewer borrowers were being turned down for mortgages at all. Gramlich contended that subprime lenders had made old-fashioned redlining a thing of the past. The new problem, he warned, was that the rise in subprime lending had been accompanied by a rising tide of predatory practices that took advantage of people with limited education or language skills—often the same immigrants and ethnic minorities who had been arbitrarily turned down for loans in the past. "The increased availability of subprime mortgage credit has created new opportunities for home ownership," he said in a speech to industry executives in 2004. "At the same time, increased subprime lending has been associated with higher levels of delinquency, foreclosure, and, in some cases, abusive lending practices."

Gramlich had privately proposed to Greenspan in 2001 that

Fed examiners scrutinize the practices of subprime lenders under their jurisdiction. Greenspan, who confirmed the conversation with Gramlich, said he had worried that the Fed examiners might be ill equipped to ferret out deceptive practices. Even worse, he said, the Fed might inadvertently give unscrupulous lenders a *Good Housekeeping* seal of approval.

In a telephone conversation three weeks before he died in September 2007, Gramlich told me he had agreed with Greenspan that the Fed's authority to swoop in as a bank examiner was murky. Gramlich also played down his conflict with Greenspan, saying it had been overblown in some press reports. Even so, Gramlich had pushed in vain for the Fed to use its authority under the Home Ownership and Equity Protection Act (HOEPA), which gave it broad power to prohibit or restrict "unfair and deceptive practices" by any kind of mortgage lender. "If I were a dictator, I would have put an end to all adjustable rate mortgages for subprime borrowers," Gramlich told me. "I think you could have done that under HOEPA."

In theory, the Fed had already used its authority to curtail much-criticized tactics, such as making loans without determining whether borrowers could plausibly repay them. But in practice, the restrictions applied only to loans with extremely high interest rates, and lenders were skillful at shifting their fees around to game the rules and stay under the limits. Less than 1 percent of all mortgages came under the rules, according to Fed officials. Fed officials openly acknowledged that their restrictions affected an insignificant share of subprime lending, but they argued as late as 2007 that the law made it difficult to rope in more lenders.

To be sure, Greenspan was ready to call for tough restrictions in some areas. The trouble was that he became obsessed by the wrong threat. Even as he demurred from using the Fed's position to tamp down the reckless lending practices of private banks and mortgage companies, he thundered in steadily more dire language against Fannie Mae and Freddie Mac, the government-sponsored mortgage companies.

Though owned by investors, Fannie and Freddie had been chartered by Congress to buy up traditional mortgages, guarantee their repayment, bundle them into securities, and resell them to investors. To hear Greenspan tell it, the two government-sponsored enterprises had become monsters that threatened to gobble up Wall Street, bankrupt the country, and destroy capitalism as we knew it. He was right that the companies posed a problem: they had become leveraged up to the eyeballs, and critics complained with some justice that they were really giant hedge funds disguised as mortgage finance companies. Because investors assumed that Congress would rescue the two companies if they got into trouble, Fannie and Freddie borrowed money at lower rates than their competitors, earned fat profits, and had built up investment portfolios totaling $1.4 trillion between them. As of May 2008, Fannie Mae had about $45 billion in core capital to cushion against losses; its investment portfolio totaled more than $700 billion, and it was guaranteeing another $2 trillion worth of mortgages held by investors.

Testifying before the Senate Committee on Banking in April 2005, Greenspan made Fannie and Freddie both sound like the man-eating plant in *Little Shop of Horrors*. He warned that the two companies posed "systemic risks for the US financial system." Their ability to borrow money more cheaply than private-sector rivals allowed them to "gain gradually but inexorably an ever-larger share of the home mortgage market," he said. He called their system a "powerful vehicle for pursuing profits" that often earned a 25 percent return—"far in excess" of the margins earned by their rivals on

Wall Street. It was "an advantage that their potential private-sector competitors cannot meet."

There were valid reasons for trying to rein in Fannie and Freddie. If something went badly wrong with the mortgage market, it was entirely possible that they might topple under the weight of their huge liabilities. And worst of all, both companies had been caught in major scandals about massaging their income statements.

Yet Fannie and Freddie were hardly the primary cause of the mortgage meltdown that would soon obliterate much of the nation's financial system. Most of their business was in traditional kinds of mortgages—full-document loans with healthy down payments and no creative twists. Shrewd analysts, like Charles Calomiris of Columbia University, later documented that the companies also bought or securitized large volumes of Alt-A mortgages. Indeed, executives at American Home said they had sold a large number of its low-doc loans to Fannie Mae. But although Fannie and Freddie had indeed bought some mortgage-backed securities backed by subprime loans, those were a small part of their holdings.

The real "systemic risk" didn't come from them. It came from the "private label" junk mortgages that the private and investment banks were creating, packaging, and often buying up themselves. When the credit markets panicked in August 2007, eventually forcing the Federal Reserve and the Treasury to prop up the banking system with more than $1 trillion in capital infusions and trillions of dollars in new lending programs, it was primarily because of the trillions of dollars in opaque mortgage-backed securities that Merrill Lynch, Citigroup, and others had created out of subprime and Alt-A mortgages.

Fannie and Freddie, far from jeopardizing the market, would later be the only players still standing. By the spring of 2008, their nemeses in the Fed and in the Bush administration would be pushing them to rescue the housing market. In a 180-degree reversal, the Fed and the Bush Treasury Department pressured Fannie and Freddie to raise more capital, guarantee bigger mortgages, and expand their portfolios.

By then, however, the losses on Wall Street were so high that the putative Little Shops of Horror were in trouble too. The deepening collapse in the housing market and rising pace of foreclosures was causing big losses from their own investment portfolios and their mortgage-backed securities. By the summer of 2008, investors were running away from the common shares of Fannie and Freddie, making it impossible for the two lenders to raise additional capital. President Bush, who had vowed that there would be no "bailouts" and who had pushed to restrain the companies, was forced to ask Congress for standby authority to lend the companies unlimited amounts of money.

"A lot of people in the country probably don't understand how important they are to the mortgage markets," the flustered president told reporters at a news conference on July 15, 2008. The Republican administration that had loathed Fannie and Freddie was suddenly so desperate that it became their best friend. Treasury Secretary Paulson memorably compared the new authority to having a "bazooka" in his pocket that he wouldn't have to use. "If you've got a squirt gun in your pocket, you may have to take it out," Paulson told a Senate hearing the same day. "If you've got a bazooka and people know you've got it, you may not have to take it out."

By early September, as it became clear that Fannie and Freddie couldn't raise fresh capital, Paulson reversed course and announced that the government would take over both companies, put them into a "conservatorship," and back them with as much as $100 billion each, if need be.

By any measure, Freddie Mac and Fannie Mae were catastrophes. Greenspan and the Bush White House had been correct in pleading with Congress to rein in their activities. At the same time, it was a canard to argue that Fannie and Freddie had been the cause of the crisis itself. As big and overextended as they were, they were much less the causes than the victims of the catastrophe that their private-sector rivals had unleashed.

To his great credit, Greenspan never claimed that the calamity would have been avoided if Congress had only heeded his advice on Fannie and Freddie. But he was deafeningly silent about the burgeoning risks building in the private sector subprime mortgage market. Greenspan's avoidance of the matter was the financial equivalent of the CIA's failure to predict the collapse of the Soviet Union or the failure of the FBI and CIA to connect the dots about al-Qaeda plans before the terrorist attacks of September 11, 2001.

Greenspan had so little to say on the subject that he barely gave the issue a nod in the first edition of his memoir, which was published in September 2007.

John Taylor, president of the National Community Reinvestment Coalition, an umbrella association of advocacy groups for low-income housing, had been trying for years to get the attention of Fed policy makers. What interested the Fed chairman, however, was not Taylor's warning about reckless lending but his occasional criticisms of Fannie Mae and Freddie Mac.

On what turned out to be the epic systemic threat to the nation's financial system, Greenspan did not seem to be interested.

By the spring of 2005, as Greenspan was nearing the end of his long tenure as Fed chairman, even he was getting worried about the housing market.

He still could not bring himself to describe the excesses in the housing market as a "bubble," but in an important turning point he admitted in a speech on May 10 that he had concerns about "froth" in many parts of the country. "Without calling the overall national issue a bubble, it's pretty clear that it's an unsustainable underlying pattern," Greenspan told the Economic Club of New York. The Fed chairman went on to acknowledge that speculative buying was apparent in places like Florida, California, Phoenix, and Las Vegas. He also admitted that a growing number of home buyers were "reaching" to finance their purchases.

Another development puzzled and worried the Fed chairman— one that few others saw as a problem. Even though the Fed had been ratcheting up the overnight federal funds rate for almost a year, the long-term interest rates that determined mortgage rates had actually edged down. Greenspan called it a "conundrum," and he didn't like it. Normally, increases in the federal funds rate prompted investors to demand higher rates on long-term Treasury bonds. He had actually been counting on such increases to help cool down the housing market.

Traditionally, a decline in long-term interest rates had been seen as an advance signal of an economic slowdown, because investors were anticipating lower demand by corporations to borrow money. That explanation didn't make sense to Greenspan, because other indicators suggested that investors were confident. Stock prices were rising, and spreads had narrowed between interest rates for supersafe Treasury bonds and much riskier bonds. Lower spreads meant that bond investors had a strong appetite for risk, signaling that they were confident. The problem with persistently low long-term rates was that the housing market might not cool down, American debt levels would continue to rise, and the country would face a higher risk of a jarring and unpleasant correction.

The maestro still wasn't worried about the explosion of subprime lending and no-document loans, or the drumbeat of complaints about abusive loan practices.

"It was clear in 2004 and even in 2003 that there were some questionable practices going on," Greenspan recalled when I sat down with him in December 2007. "But remember," he said. "It was a very small market. The big surge in subprime originations doesn't occur until 2005." Like most industry executives and analysts, Greenspan also took heart that default rates for subprime mortgages were still fairly low. "These loans came out as fairly high-priced securities, high-yielding securities, but there was very little evidence at that time that subprimes were anything other than a very good investment."

True enough, all the powerful bond-rating agencies—Moody's, Standard & Poor's, and Fitch—were assigning triple-A ratings to the vast majority of securities backed entirely by subprime and Alt-A mortgages. In addition, no one at the Fed or at the rating agencies had tried to predict what might happen to default rates if the housing boom ended—as everybody expected it would—and prices stopped climbing.

Had any of them looked hard enough, frightening evidence was available. The Center for Responsible Lending, Martin Eakes's nonprofit group, studied the default rates on subprime loans in local markets where housing prices had not been climbing. The study found that, in the absence of rising resale prices, subprime default rates had soared to a shockingly high 20 percent.

The risks were identifiable and quantifiable, but neither Greenspan nor most other bank regulators in Washington saw them coming. Yet he did seem to have an increasingly gloomy sense of foreboding that something very bad might be just over the horizon. Greenspan's gloom was apparent as central bankers and economists from around the world met in August 2005 at the Kansas City Fed's annual symposium in Jackson Hole, Wyoming.

The symposium was devoted entirely to "the Greenspan era." Alan Blinder of Princeton University, a former vice chairman of the Federal Reserve who had clashed with Greenspan, summed up the feelings of most participants. "When the score is totaled up, we think he has a legitimate claim to being the greatest central banker who ever lived," Blinder wrote in a paper with Ricardo Reis of Princeton.

Then Greenspan rose to speak, and he hardly sounded like a man reveling in accolades.

You had to translate his turgid economic jargon into ordinary English, but his underlying message was hauntingly prophetic. His basic warning was that investors and consumers alike had become too complacent about the future. They were betting too heavily on the wealth they expected to reap from soaring prices for assets— stocks, bonds, "and, most recently, homes."

"This vast increase in the market value of asset claims is in part the indirect result of investors accepting lower compensation for risk," Greenspan said. Translation: The willingness of people to keep bidding up the prices of condos in Boca Raton or Las Vegas stemmed from their unwarranted confidence about being able to resell them at even higher prices in the near future.

"Such an increase in market value is too often viewed by market participants as structural and permanent." Translation: Unfortunately, people are much too quick to believe that the easy profits they made last year mark the dawn of a permanent "new era" or "new economy."

"Financial intermediaries, of course, routinely convert capital gains in stocks, bonds, and homes into cash for businesses and households. . . . But what they perceive as newly abundant liquidity can readily disappear." Translation: Thanks to your friends at the mortgage company, you can get a home equity line of credit and turn your house into a fabulous ATM machine. But if the house loses its value and your equity looks suspect, the ATM can shut down very suddenly.

"Any onset of increased investor caution elevates risk premiums and, as a consequence, lowers asset values and promotes the liquidation of the debt that supported higher asset prices." Translation: The minute investors suddenly get worried, they will demand a higher yield or interest rate on any money they lend you for your condo. That will lower the condo's value. If the value goes down too far, you might want to "liquidate" your loan by walking away from the property.

"This is the reason that history has not dealt kindly with the aftermath of protracted periods of low risk." Translation: History shows that people who think the easy money will keep rolling in forever are likely to get clobbered.

Exactly one year later, history became a whole lot more than unkind.

6

CONNING THE CON MEN

A s exhilarating as our first foray into easy mortgages had
been, it was only when our finances spun completely out
of control that Patty and I truly tested the limits. Perhaps
fittingly, that moment came the day we got married—and wrecked
the car.

It was April 8, 2006, nearly two years since we had bought our
house. What had seemed like a brazen liar's loan in 2004 had
become genteel if not quaint by 2006. The boom in exotic mortgages was now more like an orgy of abandon that was getting closer
to its collective climax.

Merrill Lynch was pouring billions into subprime loans and hunt-
ing for a major subprime lender to buy so that it could catch up with
Bear Stearns and Lehman Brothers. Deutsche Bank had just bought
MortgageIT, a high-flying lender in New York that specialized in
Alt-A loans. Countrywide Financial, the nation's biggest mortgage

lender, was firing back by ramping up its own investment banking subsidiary to package mortgage-backed securities. With money pouring in and competition intensifying, lenders were scouring for fresh borrowers by moving even further down-market. They were approving low-doc loans for people who had just come out of bankruptcy, no-down-payment deals for people who wouldn't document their incomes, and serial mortgages to condo buyers who used their equity in one property as down payments for others. "If you can fog up a mirror, you can get a mortgage," quipped Bill Dallas, a veteran subprime lender who was then president of Ownit Mortgage Solutions in Agoura Hills, California.

It was a lucky thing for me, too. By the day of the wedding, Patty and I had emptied our savings, maxed out our credit cards, and watched our FICO scores sink into the gutter. We were about to get a tour through the underground of American finance. We would learn that people who were drowning in debt could not only borrow even more money against their homes, but also improve their credit scores in the process. We would learn how easy it was to play a notorious subprime lender against JPMorgan Chase, a supposed pillar of Wall Street respectability.

In fact, the Runyonesque hustlers in the back streets of American finance had become inseparable from the blue-blooded financial engineers on Wall Street. Sometimes they teamed up with each other. Sometimes they competed head to head. Each side was constantly trying to outsmart the other and gain market share. As the risks got higher, people on all sides were doubling down and nobody wanted to stop playing.

As our wedding day drew closer, the good news was that Patty had landed a well-paying job as an editor and was now earning $60,000 a year. She worked in a plush suite of offices in downtown Washington, and on most mornings we commuted together like a modern professional couple. To earn extra money, I was also filling in as the late editor almost every Friday night in the *Times'* Washington bureau.

The bad news was that we were drowning in even more debt than before. We didn't know how big a hole we were in, because we couldn't bear to look at the gruesome details. We knew that JPMorgan Chase was now charging 14 percent on our platinum Visa card, that SunTrust Bank was charging 22 percent on our MasterCard—and that the rates were still rising. It was a classic credit card vortex: Ballooning loan balances prompted the banks to raise their rates. Higher rates made the balances expand, which in turn made the monthly interest costs that much higher.

Still, we were full of hope about our long-awaited wedding. We had invited only two dozen people, six of whom were our children. Our old friends, Susan and Peter Kilborn, would host us at their home in Chevy Chase. Little blonde Emily, eight, would be the flower girl and had picked out a pink chiffon dress. Ben, Patty's oldest son, would escort her up the aisle. Ryan, my oldest son, would offer the first toast.

We couldn't afford a real honeymoon, but we had lined up a shoestring getaway to New York City. The *Times* let us stay for free in a one-bedroom apartment it kept for out-of-town reporters and editors. We would window-shop in SoHo, eat at out-of-the-way restaurants, and get half-price tickets to Broadway shows. For a few days, we told ourselves, we would forget about money and enjoy time with each other.

Six hours before we were set to exchange vows, Patty rammed our aging Toyota into another car while she was picking up a suit for Ben. Making matters worse, we had canceled our collision insurance to save money. We had no spare cash, but somehow we would have to pay for the repair out of our own pockets.

Cutting back on insurance was the kind of gamble that poor people made every day, and it was based on a plausible calculation. Since our eight-year-old subcompact was worth less than $4,000, the insurance premiums probably weren't worth the benefits we might or might not ever collect. It seemed like only a small gamble, but as any poor person can tell you, no bet is small if you can't afford to lose it.

Patty, smoking a Marlboro Light when I arrived at the scene of the accident, was too distraught to speak. Our little SUV had a bent front axle, a damaged front wheel, a smashed-up hood, and a wrecked grille. I coaxed it to an auto body shop a few blocks away and begged the shop owner for mercy. "It will probably cost about $2,600," he predicted, offering plenty of sympathy but not much mercy. I handed over the keys and went to dress for the wedding.

By the time we were ready to exchange our vows, I looked and felt like a wreck. I wore a navy blazer, which Patty had spruced up with a fresh pink dress shirt and a silk tie. I felt overheated and overstressed. My palms were sweaty, my face pale, my eyes glazed. The crash wouldn't be the end of the world, I knew, but it had resurrected all of my anxieties about other problems. How many last-minute wedding expenses did we still have to pay? How much money would be left once the caterers cashed their checks? How many unpaid bills for electricity, telephone, or cable TV were waiting for us back at home? How high were our credit card balances? I didn't know the answers, because I hadn't wanted to know. Now, just when I wanted to celebrate the great love of my life, all the things I hadn't wanted to know were haunting me.

Patty, by contrast, had transformed herself from a harried mother in a car accident to a shimmering goddess. As Ben escorted her up the aisle, she was dazzling and timeless. She wore a sleeveless silk dress and a chiffon wrap that left her smooth shoulders bare. Her necklace and earrings, family heirlooms, were pearls set in gold. She looked daring and sexy, yet also reminiscent of an earlier era. As she took my hand and looked at me with a smile, momentarily I felt all the tension wash away.

"Remember that God will be looking out for you," said Betsy Hague, our still-skeptical minister, after we exchanged our vows. Looking out across the room, Hague then delivered to our friends and family a message that struck me as ominous. "I want all of you who care about Patty and Ed to be there for them," she told them. "You have a role to play in their marriage too, and you have a responsibility to support them. If they go through difficult times, you need to give them strength. Just as they have been looking out for their children, you need to be there for them."

It wouldn't take long to find out how much strength we needed, and it would be far from clear that we had enough.

I felt like a crack addict calling up my dealer. We had just returned from our honeymoon in New York, and I had just reached Bob Andrews, our once and future mortgage broker, on his cell phone. "We've sold our house and moved to Denver," Bob informed me, sounding as ebullient as ever. "You and Patty should come out and visit. It's beautiful and we have plenty of room. We can all drive up into the mountains."

I was surprised at how glad I was to hear his voice. In his own way, Bob knew more about my messy life than almost anybody else. Somehow, he never seemed judgmental or condescending. Instead, he seemed to think that money trouble and failed marriages were a natural part of life, even for good people with decent jobs. I felt relieved to have the chance to unload my problems and ask for his advice.

Bob was a free spirit who had a tendency to wander in search of new excitement. With a master's in business administration, he had worked as a chief financial officer for two companies in the satellite business and he had been a turnaround consultant for several troubled companies. Bob said he had quit American Home Mortgage and moved to Denver to pursue a business deal that had something to do with copper mining and French investors. He quickly reassured me that he was still in the mortgage business and was working for a small Denver brokerage called Vertex Financial while he waited for his other deal to come through.

"Bob, we're dying over here," I wailed. "I can't even explain how it happened, but we've got these unbelievable credit card bills, and the minimum payments add up to almost $1,100 a month. There's no way we can keep that up."

I had months and months of credit card bills spread across the dining room table, and I quickly confessed the full horror of what they contained. We owed $10,474 on the MasterCard, which was tied to the "overdraft protection" plan on my account at SunTrust Bank. We owed another $18,704 on the "platinum" Visa card from JPMorgan Chase, and another $16,102 on an American Express gold card we had picked up and quickly larded with debt. We were approaching $50,000 in credit card debt alone, and it was amazing how fast and how deep we had dug ourselves in. It was even more amazing how long we had avoided the screaming evidence of a train wreck in the making.

Yet it wasn't hard to see why it had happened. Most of the debt stemmed from the long period during which Patty had struggled to find a well-paying job. Finally, after her frustrated attempts to earn money at Saks Fifth Avenue and then as a freelance editor, Patty had suddenly gotten the break that seemed to solve our problems. The Pew Research Center, a well-funded, nonpartisan policy think tank, had run across her résumé and sought her out for an interview. In November 2005, she was hired as a full-time editor with a salary of $60,000 a year. That was $20,000 more than we had figured we needed to survive, and more than she had dreamed of demanding. Even better, it was a great job that immersed Patty in exactly the kind of policy debates that fascinated her.

The problem, I told Bob, was that we had dug ourselves in so deep that even Patty's new job wouldn't be enough to rescue us. The Chase platinum card showed how fast we had lost our grip. Less than a year after accepting their 0 percent teaser rate and transferring a small balance onto the card, Chase was now charging 13.99 percent—presumably less alarming than 14 percent— and our balance at SunTrust was higher than ever, not to mention the American Express balance.

Between humongous loan balances and high rates, we had hung ourselves with the rope they had given us. In the previous December alone, we had charged $2,845 on the Chase card for Christmas gifts, food, gasoline, clothing, and other expenses. The charges included almost $350 for groceries, $700 in clothes from J. Crew, $179 at GapKids, and $700 for airplane tickets for Emily and Will to visit their father in Los Angeles. Our balance had climbed from $14,118 to $17,135, and in January 2006 we maxed out at our $19,000 credit limit. And there had been other expenses on other cards: $1,200 in dental work for Patty's son Ben; $1,600 to rent a beach house the previous year for us and all the children. Granted, the beach house was an embarrassing mistake. But given that Patty had gotten a solid job, it had seemed like an indulgence we could work off later.

Patty and I were each other's worst enablers. I was Don't Ask, and she was Don't Tell. She looked out for the household and didn't want me second-guessing her. I was tightfisted about money, but

I hated money issues and didn't want to know the details. Even Chase had become alarmed. "To help reduce your balance more quickly," it had informed us on the December bill, "your minimum payment is increased with this statement." How helpful. The minimum was now $679.

I felt foolish, ashamed, and angry as I confessed to Bob. Why had I been trying to live a lifestyle that we couldn't afford? Why had I tried to keep up the image of a conventional suburban family man, when nothing about my situation was conventional? How could I have glossed over the fact that we had been spending about $3,000 more than we were earning, month after month after month? How could a person who wrote about economics for a living fall into the kind of credit card trap that consumer groups had warned about for years?

I was furious at Patty, who often accused me of premature panic attacks and of browbeating her about our spending. But I was even angrier at myself for being a coconspirator. I hadn't returned any of the shirts she bought me at J. Crew, or boycotted any of the shows we watched on HBO, or refused to go out to dinner with her. And even though I was paying child support to my ex-wife, I had been thrilled that my boys and their friends came to our house on most days and ate many of their meals with us. Maybe I was just another pathetic and lovelorn middle-aged man, the kind who becomes enchanted by a beautiful woman and gets dumped as soon as the money runs out.

"My inclination is to just raid my 401(k) account to pay off the cards," I told Bob. "I know we'd be paying huge taxes and penalties for withdrawing money before retirement, but it's not as bad as paying all that interest to the banks."

"NO!" Bob interrupted fiercely. "You don't want to do that. You'll be paying a basic tax rate of 28 percent, and they'll hit you with another 10 percent penalty. You'd be giving up 40 percent in taxes. There's got to be a better way."

I gave Bob permission to pull a credit report on us, and he called me back an hour later. "Your credit scores have dropped quite a bit," he told me. "You had a 589 with Experian, a 596 with Equifax, and a 603 with TransUnion. We need to get your scores back above 620." Bob carefully avoided using the word "subprime," which sounded unclean and untrustworthy. It didn't matter. In the eyes of the mortgage industry, I was deep in subprime territory. By one measure, I was in the bottom 20 percent of Americans on creditworthiness. I was ashamed.

From Bob's standpoint, the issue had nothing to do with whether I was good or bad, shifty or honorable. It was just a pragmatic challenge: was there a way I could refinance my house and pay off my credit cards without ending up in even more trouble than I was already in? By the next day, he had come up with a scheme that was either wickedly smart or proof that the big-money people had become delirious. Or both.

"What we're going to do is a two-step plan," he announced. "The bad news is that your credit scores are down, so we can't just do a simple refinance. But the good news is that you've owned your house for a year and a half, and it's gone up in value. So you can borrow against the equity. So in the first step of the plan, we're going to get you a really ugly mortgage that is big enough to pay off all your credit cards."

"OK, I'm with you so far," I said uncertainly.

"OK. Now, because this mortgage is really ugly, your monthly payments will jump to about $3,700. As I said, this is a really ugly loan. But don't worry about it, because you're only going to stay in it for about three months. Once we pay off your credit cards, your credit scores will go up and we can get you a cheaper loan."

The way Bob figured it, my monthly payment would be down to about $3,200 by the fall. The "ugly" loan would effectively cost me an extra $1,100 while I had it, but I would save several hundred dollars every month after that. The new mortgage would still be $600 more than my current mortgage because it would include all my credit card debt, but it would be at least $600 a month less than the combined total of what I was paying between the mortgage and credit cards right then. And mortgage interest, unlike interest on credit card debt, is entirely tax-deductible.

"That's bizarre," I said. "Why should I qualify for a better mortgage? Anybody would be able to tell that I had just been drowning in debt. Won't it be obvious that I have just as much debt as before? Why would anybody think I was a safer risk?"

"The reason is that your credit scores are being hurt by your high loan balances," Bob answered. "Banks don't like to see people with high loan balances, because it's a sign they're in trouble."

Amen to that. But wouldn't I have even more debt than before?

Bob tried to be patient. He didn't get many customers who seemed alarmed that their credit scores were about to go up. "As soon as your loan balances are back down, they stop penalizing you and your credit scores go back up," he said. And there was a quirk in the system: after about three months, my credit reports would show that there had been a "high balance" on my credit cards, but no one would know when it had occurred. All the new lender would see was a clean bill of health on my current credit cards.

I tried to wrap my mind around all this.

- A borrower who is obviously drowning in debt in June borrows another $50,000 and boosts his creditworthiness by September.
- The borrower has at least as much debt as before, but instead of being maxed out on his credit cards, he is maxed out on his house.

- The borrower probably has even more debt than before, because the refinancing costs will be paid from the proceeds of the bigger mortgage.
- The borrower still has all the same credit cards, so he can go out and max up to the limits all over again.

"That's about the size of it," said Bob. In fact, the credit bureaus allowed people like Bob to calculate exactly how much my credit score would jump if I eliminated my credit card balances. Bob faxed me my credit reports, complete with "What if?" calculations. Each of the three bureaus came up with a slightly different estimate, but they all calculated that my score would jump from about 590 to between 620 and 640.

The whole scheme was insane, but it worked exactly as Bob had predicted. Within a few weeks, an appraiser had valued our house at $505,000, almost 10 percent above the original purchase price two years earlier. On June 12, Patty and I signed a new mortgage for $472,000 with Fremont Investment & Loan in Santa Monica, California. Fremont was the fourth-largest subprime lender in the country in 2006, and it had a horrendous reputation. Less than a year later, the attorney general of Massachusetts would sue it for abusive lending practices, and the state supreme court eventually prohibited Fremont from foreclosing on many of its loans. (In December 2008, the court upheld the injunction against foreclosures, declaring that Fremont should have known that no-money-down loans with low initial "teaser" rates would be impossible for many borrowers to repay.) The Federal Deposit Insurance Corporation, meanwhile, accused it of reckless lending and issued a cease-and-desist order in the spring of 2007 that essentially forced it out of business.

Just as Bob had predicted, Fremont gave us a very expensive loan. Our monthly payment jumped to $3,700 from $2,600. That was nothing. If we kept the mortgage for two years, the interest rate would jump as high as 11.5 percent and the monthly payments would ratchet up to as high as $4,500. It was one of those infamous "2/28" mortgages—offering a comparatively low rate that was fixed for two years, followed by a much higher adjustable rate after that.

Normally, subprime lenders tried to lock borrowers into their loans for up to three years by charging them "prepayment penalties" totaling thousands of dollars if they tried to refinance. Fremont would waive the prepayment penalty if a person agreed to pay an additional "point"—1 percent of the loan amount—or $4,722 in my case. Bob arranged for me to pay the point, but I paid for it with money borrowed through the refinancing.

None of this came cheap. I had paid about $5,800 in fees to Vertex Financial, Bob's mortgage company, and to the settlement company. On top of that, Fremont had paid Vertex a sales commission—known as a "yield-spread premium"—of $4,698. Yield-spread premiums were one of the subprime industry's favorite tactics for charging steep sales fees that most borrowers didn't notice. The fee didn't come out of my pocket immediately, but I would be paying it in the form of a higher interest rate.

The paperwork was so confusing that I was never exactly sure who was paying what. I hazily understood that I was paying most of the fees, one way or another, but I couldn't figure out how and I couldn't see any better alternatives. Patty and I paid off our credit cards and my credit scores jumped. In October 2006, Bob refinanced us once again with JPMorgan Chase. In its own way, this was poetic: I had replaced the outrageous rates of our Chase platinum credit card with the substantially lower rate charged by Chase Home Finance.

At first glance, JPMorgan Chase and Fremont seemed to be in completely different worlds. J. P. Morgan himself had almost single-handedly saved the banking industry from collapse in 1907, corralling all the big executives into a room and getting them to agree on a plan to lend money to each other. As an institution, JPMorgan Chase (the merger with Chase Manhattan Bank took place in 2000) was one of the few banks that had avoided getting stuck with billions of bad mortgages on its books.

That didn't mean JPMorgan didn't make sleazy loans or package them into mortgage-backed securities, of course. It was one of the biggest subprime lenders in South Florida, an area that encompasses Miami, Fort Lauderdale, and Palm Beach and that later became one of the epicenters of the foreclosure meltdown. It was also a big buyer and reseller of such loans. Indeed, JPMorgan was both a customer of Fremont, buying up thousands of its subprime mortgages, and a head-to-head rival that made its own skanky loans.

"People say, 'Oh, subprime,' like they're some kind of disease," Tom Kelly, a spokesman for JPMorgan Chase, told the *South Florida Sun-Sentinel*. "Subprime can mean responsible borrowers . . . it might just be that they made a very low down payment or they were late on a few credit card payments."

I realized later that JPMorgan Chase, the supposed pillar of respectability, had skinned me twice as much as Fremont. My mortgage papers revealed that it had paid Bob and his brokerage firm almost $10,000—twice as much as Fremont had. That implied that JPMorgan might not have been as shrewd as Fremont about what it really had to pay for a customer like me. What I knew for sure is that I was ultimately paying that sales commission, through yet another hidden premium tacked onto my interest rate.

JPMorgan Chase was hardly the only "respectable" name that played in the same sandbox as Fremont. So did Goldman Sachs, Merrill Lynch, Lehman Brothers, Bear Stearns, Morgan Stanley, and every other big firm. So, too, did giant hedge funds, like Elling-ton Management, that traded mortgages and mortgage-backed securities on every level. They were all buying up junk loans from Fremont and other subprime lenders as fast as they could. "As long as Wall Street wanted to buy the mortgages, we were going to keep making them," Kyle Walker, who was Fremont's president at the time, told me later.

But there was a more ominous lesson. Just as Patty and I had staved off disaster by borrowing even more against the house, millions of people were using rapid-fire refinancing to escape the payment shock that would come when their initial "teaser rates" expired.

To investors, the remarkable thing about subprime mortgages was the low default rate. A study by the Federal Reserve Bank of Boston showed that the vast majority of subprime borrowers in New England paid off their mortgages in less than three years. However, that was possible only if home prices were going up and borrowers could refinance their homes or sell them. For many people, including Patty and me, the financial machinations only postponed the day of reckoning. If home prices stopped climbing, that day would arrive very abruptly.

In our case, the money problems were beginning to pull us apart. We had already abandoned plans for a summer vacation in 2006, partly to offset the cost of our wedding. The intense love we felt for each other was being supplanted faster than we ever imagined pos-sible by raw feelings of fear, suspicion, anger, and resentment.

"We can't keep racking up debt like this," I told her one night, annoyed that she didn't appear to share my urgency. "Even with your job, we're spending way more than we make every month. If we keep this up, we'll lose the house."

"Aaach, there you go again," Patty snapped. "Why is it that every time you look at a bill you act as if the world were coming to an end? I am doing what I can to make money, and to spend as little as possible. I know better than anyone that we have money problems, but it is not the end of the world. You act as if I'm not taking this seriously unless I get as hysterical as you."

"What the fuck are you talking about?" I exploded. "Maybe you don't understand, but this is a simple question of math. We're running deeper into debt every month. It's not as though I'm crazy or that I'm imagining all this."

"Don't talk to me like that," she snapped. "I put myself through college entirely on my own. You have no clue what having no money is like. What it actually means to be poor. Do you think I'm not as worried about money as you are? How does it help to get hysterical and attack me? I'm sick of it. This isn't what I signed up for."

Now I was feeling betrayed. "I have put everything I have on the line for you. I have racked up $50,000 in additional debt since we moved into the house. How could I possibly have committed myself to you any more than I have?"

"*Your* debt?" she spat back. "Why are you calling it *your* debt? It's *our* debt."

That stopped me. Of all the things to fight about, why would Patty focus her wrath on whether I was claiming all the debt for myself? I didn't care whether it was my debt or our debt. If she wanted a bigger share of the burden, she was welcome to as much as she wanted. To Patty, I seemed to be using money—in the form of debt—to wield power. "By calling it your debt, you're negating the fact that I was taking equal responsibility," she said. "It's not as if I was racking up the debt because I didn't think I would be on the hook for it. I want to be viewed as an equal partner."

Patty prided herself on her independence. She had repeatedly battled her father, a charismatic physician with a volcanic temper who had intimidated her and beaten her as a child. Halfway through Patty's freshman year in college at the University of Redlands in California, her father had stopped paying her tuition costs and living expenses. Patty paid her own way through college by working as a waitress. Now, as the two of us grappled with our own financial woes, I suddenly seemed disturbingly reminiscent of her father.

We seemed to be on different planets, each of us panicking about a different problem. For me, it was all about the money. I might have preferred living in an apartment or making other sacrifices to keep my spending in line with my income, but now that we were in this house I wanted to make it work.

"I have never been as baffled by anyone as I have been by you," I told her. I didn't feel like a power-hungry autocrat. I felt frightened and powerless, dependent on her for my financial survival. It seemed to me that we both had the same goals—more money and less debt. What was so hard about coming up with a strategy to make that happen?

For Patty, it was all about the fear of being trapped. She was aching that I seemed to view her as a burden, and furious that I seemed to be blaming her for our problems. Instead of offering the hope of real love after a long and troubled marriage, I seemed to have morphed into an ill-tempered ogre. She hadn't pretended to have any money when we fell in love, yet now I seemed to have turned the tables, expecting her to transform herself into a high-earning, rat-race professional. When I didn't get my way, I exploded in rage.

"What have I done?" she wailed during one fight. "What have I gotten myself into? I have to get out of here."

7

IN SEARCH OF THE
SMART MONEY

Why was Fremont Investment & Loan willing to loan almost a half-million dollars to me? Or, better yet, *how* had Fremont been able to loan me the money?

It was an open secret that lenders like Fremont weren't going to lose money if I defaulted. Fremont sold off its mortgages as fast as it could, usually to Wall Street firms that bundled them into securities. The investors who bought the securities were the ones with money on the line.

That just begged the question, though: why were investors so eager to buy a piece of my mortgage? These weren't the kind of cowboy day traders who had helped fuel the dot-com bubble. These were professional asset managers at pension funds, insurance companies, college endowments, hedge funds, and big foreign banks around the world. This was the smart money.

At Fremont's headquarters in Santa Monica, just a few blocks from the beach, Kyle Walker may have been wondering about the same question. At the time we got our Fremont loan in June 2006, Walker, forty-five, had just been promoted from chief operating officer to president. With dark hair, a square jaw, and an athletic build, he had Hollywood good looks and came across as low-key, sober, and straightforward—strikingly at odds with Fremont's usual customers.

Walker had spent his entire career in southern California's subprime industry, and he had worked at some of Orange County's earliest lenders. He had seen his share of housing booms and busts, and he had seen high-flying lenders crash and burn. Indeed, the industry had enjoyed its first phase of rapid growth during the mid-1990s, only to be nearly wiped out when credit markets seized up in 1998 and 1999 as a result of the Russian financial crisis and the shudders surrounding the collapse of Long-Term Capital Management, the hedge fund. What Los Angeles lacked in variety for weather, it made up for in financial volatility.

Walker had joined Fremont in 1994. As head of its consumer lending business, he had engineered much of Fremont's transformation from a sleepy bank that specialized in consumer installment loans—cars, satellite TV dishes, Jacuzzis—into a powerhouse subprime mortgage lender.

By the time I became a customer, Fremont was an aggressive and unapologetic bottom-feeder of the industry. It focused on scary loans to scary customers, and it charged steep fees and interest rates. As a "wholesale" lender, it didn't deal directly with customers. Instead, it bought loans from thousands of independent mortgage brokers, many of whom were honest but plenty of whom were just quick-buck artists. For a while, Fremont's profit margins were often fatter than those of better-known rivals like Countrywide or New Century. By 2006, even Walker was amazed at how much money was flowing from Wall Street, and how easy the terms had become.

"Everybody was a real estate investor," Walker told me when I tracked him down much later. "I even had my goofy gardener come and tell me, in broken English, that he was buying houses in Phoenix with 100 percent LTV [loan-to-value] loans. Buying houses in Phoenix with 100 percent loans!"

Wall Street firms and banks from around the country eagerly bought what Fremont had to sell. "We were known on Wall Street as a Tier One lender, a preferred originator with a long history," Walker said.

As the housing bubble neared its peak, more and more lenders were chasing the same number of borrowers. The competition for new loans had intensified, so the lenders were lowering their standards. "You'd hear that somebody down the street was offering 95 percent loans, and you'd say, 'How the hell are they doing 95's?,'" Walker said. "So you'd call the Lehman guys and the Goldman guys and the Merrills, and ask them, 'Are you securitizing 95's?'"

"The first one would say no and the second one would say no," Walker continued, "but then somebody would say yes. And when you started to do 95 percent loans, the performance would be good. So then someone would say, how about doing 100 percent? It just kept stretching further."

I told Walker my story, and he didn't blink. People like Patty and me were the bread and butter of Fremont's business. The only thing that seemed to make him wince was that we had been able to bail out of our mortgage after only three months. We had gotten out so quickly that Fremont didn't have time to sell off the mortgage. "It probably wasn't profitable for us," said Walker, after mulling over the story. He seemed philosophical. Sometimes you won, and sometimes you lost. It was all in the percentages. "If you paid us the point and our fees," he said, "it would be OK."

But what kind of investors would have wanted a piece of my $472,000 loan from Fremont? The overworked cliché among policy makers and industry pundits was that too many people were making loans and selling them without having any "skin in the game." But institutional investors weren't supposed to be stupid, and securitizing mortgages wasn't a new idea. Fannie Mae and Freddie Mac had been doing it for decades, and banks all over the world had been buying their securities.

I could imagine that some Chinese conglomerate, bulging with extra dollars from exports to the United States, might love my dodgy loan because I was paying a higher interest rate. But would it love my loan so much that it would accept an interest rate almost as low as what it could get on US Treasury bills?

The answer was yes, and the reason was financial alchemy. It was an alchemy that transformed subprime loans like mine into securities with the same triple-A ratings as US Treasuries. If it seemed improbable at first glance, it was absurd on closer inspection. But the transformation was so popular that investors snapped up nearly $1 trillion worth of triple-A bonds backed by subprime and Alt-A mortgages in 2006 alone.

To see how this worked, I decided to track the course of a pool of Fremont mortgages called "JPMAC 2006-FRE1." FRE1 was a bundle of nearly $1 billion in mortgages that Fremont had sold to JPMorgan Chase and that JPMorgan Chase had resold as securities in January 2006.

A quick glance at the prospectus for FRE1 confirmed that the loans were truly creepy, made to borrowers with bad credit, many of whom weren't documenting their incomes and weren't putting any money down. In other words, they were like me. In spite of all this, there it was in black and white: 80 percent of the bonds for FRE1 had been rated triple-A—the gold standard for safety—by Fitch, Moody's, and Standard & Poor's. Befitting the apparently terrific quality of these securities, JPMorgan had offered investors less than one-half of a percentage point above LIBOR, the daily index of the rates that top banks charged each other on overnight loans.

Somebody had gotten fleeced, and it wasn't me.

The sexed-up new securities were amazing in their intricacy and in their mathematical modeling. The bonds were divided into "tranches," or slices, so that investors could choose their preferred balance between risk and return. In addition to being sliced, the risk had been diced, thanks to a slew of abstruse protections: "overcollateralization," "subordination," "yield maintenance agreements," "repurchase agreements," and "credit enhancement." The more you looked at the incredible complexity of the cross-protections, the more dubious they seemed. The last time I had heard about credit enhancement, I was enhancing my own credit scores by borrowing an extra $60,000. But that had been a scam. Was it really possible to turn toxic sludge into gold? And even if you could engineer all the risk out of these mortgages, why bother? If you wanted the safety of Treasuries, why not just buy the damn Treasuries?

As far as the major rating agencies were concerned, the gold was real. Standard & Poor's, Moody's Investors Service, and Fitch Ratings had each rated 80 percent of these securities as triple-A, meaning they were as close to risk-free as you could get. A full 95 percent of the securities were rated A or higher. The last 5 percent were rated BBB or lower.

Amazingly, investors were so hot for these "triple-A" subprime bonds that, despite having watched the lenders gut their standards to produce a bonanza of iffy mortgages, Wall Street firms literally couldn't buy up enough mortgages to meet demand. To deal with the shortfall, they began conjuring up billions of dollars' worth of "synthetic" securities that didn't contain any mortgages at all. These pseudosecurities were backed by financial instruments called credit-default swaps, which were insurance contracts against the default of pools like FRE1.

JPMorgan Chase had been buying and securitizing billions of dollars of Fremont mortgages, as had all the other big Wall Street firms. Nobody seemed to care that disgruntled borrowers regularly sued Fremont, charging that they had been deceived about their loans, or that a growing number of institutional investors were demanding their money back on Fremont loans that had gone sour.

Personally, I had been an entirely satisfied customer. The company had loaned me the money I wanted, and it hadn't made me jump through a lot of hoops or given me a hard time. When I abruptly paid off my loan in just three months—which Fremont had *not* wanted me to do—nobody whined or tried to stop me. In fact, a Fremont representative called me a few months later, politely inquiring why I hadn't cashed a $400 refund it had sent to clear out my old escrow account. I sheepishly admitted I had forgotten.

The prospectus for JPMAC 2006-FRE1 spelled out in lascivious detail just how nasty the Fremont mortgages were. Right at the top, it warned that the foreclosure rate was likely to be "substantially higher" for these loans than for traditional mortgages. It said the borrowers had "imperfect" credit histories and that some of them had been through recent bankruptcies and foreclosures. The average credit score was 627, 33 points below the lowest possible level for a "prime" customer. Many borrowers' scores were a lot lower than that.

For anyone seeking gorier details, Fremont sorted the borrowers according to a scoring system of A+ through D. The good news was that 85 percent of the 4,956 borrowers in this pool were A+. The bad news was that you could qualify for an A+ even if you had been in bankruptcy just two years earlier. The pool also had 90 B borrowers, which meant they could have been in bankruptcy as recently as eighteen months earlier. It even had 16 C– borrowers, who could have gotten out of bankruptcy the day before their mortgage was approved.

Back in the Stone Age—say, around 2000—damaged credit alone would have been as much risk as most battle-hardened lenders would stomach at one time. In 2006, by contrast, "imperfect" credit histories were just the start. Forty-three percent of the borrowers in FRE1 had also taken out "stated-income" liar's loans. Half of its borrowers had taken out piggyback second mortgages, which usually meant they were buying houses with no money down. On average, the combined "loan-to-value ratio" for people with piggyback loans was 98 percent; they had no equity.

Industry executives called this a "layering of risks." It was more like a surefire formula for losing money: You make loans exclusively to troubled borrowers, give them an open invitation to lie about their incomes, and let them borrow the full purchase price of a house without putting any money down. Hmm. Bad history, no income, no documentation, and none of the borrower's money on the line. What could go wrong?

As it happened, things were already going wrong. The prospectus noted that Fremont's overall foreclosure rate, though still low, had more than doubled from 1.05 percent in 2002 to 2.31 percent in 2004. And that was at a time when the economy and the housing market were both still roaring. It was a good bet that the foreclosure rates would climb a lot higher. Almost all the borrowers had "teaser" rates that would jump sharply after two years and were likely to keep climbing in the years to come. The actual increases would depend on prevailing interest rates, but the maximum possible rate for these borrowers was, on average, a frightening 13.42 percent.

So what explained the triple-A ratings?

That was where the miracle of securitization came in. Like most other practices at the heart of the housing bubble, securitization was a valid financing tool that had been stretched to impossible extremes. The original idea was to take a pool of debt and slice up the risk to suit different investor appetites. People who wanted safety bought "senior" bonds that paid a lower interest rate but would be the first investors to get their money back. People who wanted higher returns bought "subordinated" bonds that were riskier because they would have to absorb the first losses from any defaults. It was a little tricky, but the basic idea made sense. If you could parcel out the risk to investors with different appetites for it, you could tap into a bigger pool of capital and probably borrow money at lower rates.

Securitizing subprime mortgages from Fremont and its rivals, however, was a whole different story from securitizing traditional thirty-year loans. The newest mortgages were so risky that any honest reckoning would require a lender to charge astronomically high interest rates. If that had happened, nobody would have wanted the loans and that would have been the end of the story. To avoid that pitfall, the financial engineers had to climb to a much higher level of complexity and obfuscation.

In the FRE1 pool, the four triple-A tranches offered bonds totaling $756 million. Even in non-subprime pools, these "senior" or "super senior" bonds came with a number of special privileges. If the pool started losing money as a result of defaults, the losses would all be assigned to the bondholders at the bottom of the ladder. The senior-bond holders wouldn't suffer any losses until the 20 percent of bondholders at the bottom had been wiped out. In addition, if borrowers paid off their loans ahead of time, because they had either sold their houses or refinanced, the first rounds of principal repayment would be distributed to the senior-bond holders.

It was complicated, but the basic idea was simple: the high-risk bondholders at the bottom of the pool, who received the highest interest rates, were the first ones to take any losses and the last ones to get all their money back. As long as the losses didn't add up to more than 20 percent of the total pool, nobody at the top would lose a dime. The rating agencies were convinced that the worst-case scenario was that losses would hit 6 percent, making the top-level tranches seem safe.

Subprime mortgages were so risky that tranching alone didn't provide enough safety to clinch the coveted triple-A rating, so top bondholders received a slew of other protections. The big requirement was "overcollateralization," which was a complicated formula to channel some of those high-interest payments from borrowers into extra collateral. If all went well, the tiny tranches at the bottom would become fatter over time and better able to absorb defaults.

Behind all that was another form of protection: default insurance. Some of it was buried in the mortgages themselves, in the form of insurance policies that the lenders took out to protect their investors; some of it was wrapped up in the securities, through instruments called credit-default swaps; and an awful lot of it was just floating out there in the marketplace, more as a way to speculate than to reduce risk.

Of all those forms of insurance, the biggest and hottest business was in credit-default swaps. These were financial contracts sold by bond insurers, the most notorious of which became American International Group, or AIG. With a credit-default swap, the insurance company sold a contract to cover an investor's loss in the event that a particular mortgage-backed security went into default. If one of the rating agencies lowered its rating for that security, the insurer usually had to pay money to the investor to make up for the increase in risk. If the security defaulted, the insurer would be on the hook for everything.

The party didn't stop there. Credit-default swaps became a sensation among traders as instruments for betting on the underlying mortgage securities. It didn't matter whether you owned the underlying mortgage-backed security. If you owned the credit-default swap, you were entitled to be paid off in the event of default. The ability to buy the insurance without owning the bond led to an explosion in the popularity of credit-default swaps as an alternative means of betting on subprime mortgages. The result was an exponential growth in the creation and trading of new swaps. The nominal value of the subprime-based swap trading ballooned into the trillions of dollars. There was literally no limit to how many of them you could create, assuming people wanted to buy them. And people did. Because the trading value of credit-default swaps mirrored the market value of the mortgage-backed securities, they were used to create "synthetic" mortgage-backed securities that could let even more investors bet on the future of the market.

It was anybody's guess how safe you were after all the crisscrossing protection was put into place. Safe or not, the rating agencies bought the story, and investors bought the bonds. The triple-A bondholders in FRE1 would get only 0.4 percent above LIBOR. Investors in the "M-11" tranche at the bottom would get 3.75 percent above LIBOR.

To wrap my head around the concept of triple-A subprime mortgages, I phoned up Frank Pallotta, a friend who had been a managing director at Morgan Stanley and who had been trading mortgages and mortgage-backed securities for years. At least he had been until early 2008, when the mortgage market collapsed. These days, Pallotta was working from his home as a consultant to investors and sometimes to the federal government. Frank and I had met in Las Vegas at a securitization conference, and he didn't mind tutoring me on how this stuff worked.

"Nobody's saying that the mortgages themselves are as safe as Treasuries," he explained to me, as I puzzled over the FRE1. The issue, he said, was how much "support" the bondholders at the top layers were getting from the ones below them. If you thought a pool of subprime loans could have losses of about 6 percent, and the top bondholders were shielded from the first 20 percent of losses, then the bonds at the top should be safe even if the underlying mortgages weren't. It wasn't unreasonable to rate those bonds triple-A.

"The problem wasn't that some of these securities had triple-A ratings," Pallotta said. "The problem was in how much support those bonds were getting to justify the triple-A ratings. If you had the worst deal in the world, you might have 99 percent subordination supporting the top 1 percent. But that top slice would still be triple-A."

The complexity masked the real problem: there was no reliable historical data about how subprime loans performed. Subprime mortgages had barely existed ten years earlier, and the ones that had existed at that time were tame compared to the ones being made in 2005. Nobody knew if the losses in a housing downturn would be 6 percent, 20 percent, or higher. Worse yet, all the risk models assumed that home prices would keep climbing, at least slowly. This assumption was based on decades of data showing that, on a national basis, average home prices had barely ever suffered an annual decline since the Great Depression.

In a detailed paper that he presented at a Federal Reserve symposium in 2008, Gary Gorton of the Yale School of Management argued that the assumption of rising home prices was built into the very structure of both subprime mortgages and the securities behind them. "What made these mortgages and these securities so different is that they were all based on the idea of rising home prices," Gorton told me. Gorton had himself worked as a consultant, modeling new debt securities for financial companies. This was a huge break from the past. In a bubble market, subprime lenders weren't betting on the borrowers. They were betting on the rising value of the collateral.

The weird science was just beginning. Thanks to another raft of financial engineers, Fremont's bundle of mortgages underwent a second round of alchemy that was even more surreal than the first. It was time for "collateralized debt obligations."

Why bother with a second round of alchemy? Because in order to make a subprime deal work, it wasn't enough to sell the triple-A slices that had been shined up and deodorized. You also had to sell the raunch-tranche at the bottom, and those were much nastier than original Fremont mortgages themselves. If nobody bought the malodorous 20 percent of bonds with all the risk, there wouldn't be anybody to shield those who bought the top 80 percent. Unfortunately, and contrary to what investors had come to believe, shifting the risk from one spot to another didn't mean it had disappeared. "It's the law of conservation of misery," said Tanya Styblo Beder, head of SBCC Group, a consulting firm that specializes in securitization. "You can move the misery around, but it never goes away."

JPMorgan had absolutely no trouble selling Fremont's misery. Its buyers included hedge funds like Ellington Management; Wall Street firms like Lehman Brothers; and foreign banks like Royal

Bank of Canada, Gulf International Bank in Bahrain, and Fortis Bank in Belgium. All of these institutions had created "mezzanine collateralized debt obligations," or "mezz CDOs," to buy up the raunch-tranches of subprime pools like FRE1.

A collateralized debt obligation was basically another pool like FRE1, with a similar structure of dividing risk into different slices. The difference was that a CDO generally bought the *securities* backed by subprime mortgages instead of buying subprime mortgages themselves. A mezz CDO focused specifically on the super-risky layers that one would have thought nobody wanted. CDOs had been around for more than a decade, but it wasn't until about 2002 that they started being used to finance mortgages. By 2006, as housing prices and subprime mortgages were both peaking, financial companies were cranking out more than $200 billion worth of new CDOs a year, according to JPMorgan.

What made the mezz CDOs so amazing was the way they repeated the same alchemy that JPMorgan Chase had used initially to create FRE1. Consider the case of something called Libertas Preferred Funding III, a CDO that started out with about $633 million in assets and had several million dollars' worth of FRE1's raunch-tranches. Libertas III was the creation of a Philadelphia-based investment boutique called Cohen & Company. The fund had the unwanted slices from a rogues' gallery of other lenders: Countrywide, IndyMac, New Century, Option One, First Franklin, and many others.

In other words, Libertas III contained the worst of the worst. So did its cousins, Libertas Preferred Funding I through V. Yet just like FRE1, about 80 percent of its bonds received triple-A ratings from Moody's, S&P, and Fitch in March 2006.

This seemed like more than alchemy. It was magic: JPMorgan Chase had turned the worst of the worst into the best of the best.

Libertas actually outdid JPMorgan in its incantations about safety, offering not just "senior" but "super senior" securities in its top tranche. Super senior. The mind reeled at the thought.

Who were these guys at Libertas? CDO issuers were a lot more secretive than the issuers of ordinary mortgage-backed securities, and they were usually based in offshore tax havens. They were not required to disclose financial information in public filings with the Securities and Exchange Commission, because they only sold their securities through private placements to big institutional investors. In fact, it was hard for an ordinary person to even know what a CDO was holding. Investors had to sign secrecy agreements before getting a look at a prospectus. Fortunately for me, Libertas III had defaulted on the covenants with its bondholders and was being liquidated in the summer of 2008. The liquidators had published a legal notice listing all its assets, which I read scrupulously.

Officially, Libertas III was headquartered in the Cayman Islands. In practice, it was run by Cohen & Company, based in Philadelphia. Founded in 2000, Cohen & Company specialized in creating complex financial products that most people had never heard about. Cohen wasn't well known outside the cloistered world of "structured finance," but its chief financial wizard was at the very center of the alchemy machine.

That wizard was Christopher Ricciardi, a thirty-something financial engineer who had been one of the principal architects of Merrill Lynch's massive and ultimately disastrous gamble on mortgage-backed CDOs. A graduate of the University of Richmond and the Wharton School of Business, Ricciardi had been around in the early days of CDOs, when they were used primarily to help package industrial and commercial loans. He had started as a mortgage trader at Prudential Securities, then hopped to Credit Suisse and then to Merrill Lynch in 2003.

At Merrill, Ricciardi had become managing director for "global structured credit products," which put him in charge of asset-backed securities and CDOs. Ricciardi had turned Merrill into the country's biggest single producer of CDOs in 2003, 2004, and 2005. Merrill sold $40 billion worth of them in 2004 and 2005 alone. In February 2006, Ricciardi had quit Merrill and accepted Daniel Cohen's offer to become chief executive of Cohen & Company.

At Cohen, Ricciardi repeated the growth he had achieved at Merrill, propelling Cohen to the top ranks of CDO producers as well. By early 2008, Cohen claimed to be managing about $40 billion, up from $10 billion two years earlier. Most of that was through CDOs. Unfortunately for Ricciardi, many of Cohen's CDOs are dead in the water. Libertas III defaulted on its bonds in June 2008, and creditors began liquidating in August. The other four Libertas CDOs were in various stages of default as well, with many of their "AAA" tranches slashed to "CCC."

Ricciardi left Merrill Lynch long before it began to implode, but his legacy was crucial to what nearly destroyed it. The catastrophe began in 2007, when panic about subprime default rates led to panic about mortgage-backed securities. Merrill was caught holding tens of billions of CDOs that nobody wanted to buy. It wrote off $8 billion in mortgage-related losses in October 2007, and CEO Stan O'Neal was forced to resign a few days later. On July 30, 2008, Merrill announced that it had sold $30 billion in CDOs for just twenty-two cents on the dollar to a Dallas-based money manager. On September 14, 2008, as Lehman Brothers was collapsing, Merrill Lynch reached a hasty deal to sell itself to Bank of America.

Ricciardi was still running Cohen & Company from his office on Park Avenue at the end of 2008, but neither he nor Daniel Cohen, the chairman of Cohen & Company, would talk to me. From what I could tell, Ricciardi was still a believer in CDOs. In September

2008 he published an "open letter" to Treasury Secretary Henry M. Paulson Jr. on how to fix the financial system. "Where securitization went wrong in recent years was with subprime mortgages," Ricciardi wrote, acknowledging that those investments had performed "disastrously." But he expressed shock that investors had become "irrational" and fled from all kinds of securitizations, not just the ones tied to subprime mortgages. "The true cause of the credit crisis has been the wholesale and irrational shutdown of the securitization market," he wrote.

Fortunately, Ricciardi had a solution. Institutional bond managers and hedge funds had billions of dollars to invest in mortgage-backed securities again, he argued. All they needed was to regain the ability to borrow money, so they could generate "acceptable" returns. This was where it got interesting. "In the absence of a way to finance the purchase of these assets, such funds must bid at prices which represent an attractive absolute return acceptable to their investors (15% to 25%, typically)," Ricciardi wrote.

That was an eye-opener. An annual return of 15–25 percent sounded spectacular to me, but apparently it was just par for the smart money. What Ricciardi seemed to be saying, though, was that to get an "acceptable return" you needed to turbocharge the investment through borrowing. And nobody wanted to lend money for that kind of purchase, in part because the private insurers and credit-default swap people had been nearly wiped out. Ricciardi's proposal: the government could step in and offer its own guarantees or default insurance on triple-A securitizations. The government could create a new "Federal Bond Insurance Corporation." "Once you add a government guaranty, investors are willing to purchase, trade, finance, and easily mark to market," he wrote. Not only that, but it would pose little risk to taxpayers.

"The FBIC would be subject to losses only in the most extreme of scenarios."

It was a perfect idea. Since the private bond insurers had nearly been wiped out by providing guarantees on subprime mortgages, the government would take their place. Investors could swoop back in, confident of once again earning an "acceptable" return.

Why hadn't I thought of that?

Bill Ackman, founder of Pershing Square Capital, a hedge fund in New York City, had been thinking a lot about the alchemy of subprime mortgages. By the start of 2007, he was convinced that a catastrophe was coming and that he could make money on it.

Ackman, 41, didn't claim to be an expert in the intricacies of CDOs and other arcane mortgage-backed securities. At heart he was a generalist who looked for opportunities by either shaking up underperforming companies or selling short their shares. His targets had included Sears Holdings Corporation, McDonald's Corporation, and Target Corporation.

Ackman had taken a keen interest in the housing and mortgage markets because they dovetailed with a battle he had been waging since 2002 against the nation's big bond insurers. The bond insurers, like MBIA Inc. and Ambac Financial Group, insured investors against losses if bond issuers defaulted on their obligations. Ackman had accused the companies for years of having far too little capital to cover their risks from corporate and municipal bonds. As default rates on subprime mortgages began climbing in 2006, he warned that insurers faced an even bigger potential catastrophe with all the mortgage-backed securities they had insured.

Delinquency and default rates were shooting up higher than the rating agencies had assumed. Many lenders were seeing a new spike in "early payment defaults"—borrowers falling behind within the first three months. In places like Miami and Las Vegas, condo flippers were walking away from properties without even making a first payment. Bill Dallas's Ownit Mortgage Solutions had abruptly shut its doors in December 2006. New Century Financial, in Irvine, filed for bankruptcy in April 2007.

On May 24, 2007, Ackman tried to connect all the dots in a speech called "Who's Holding the Bag?" He warned that almost every player in the mortgage boom had been trying to pass the risk on to someone else. Precisely because people at each link in the chain thought they were safe, he continued, they were all taking bigger risks and setting the stage for an epic meltdown. He began by outlining the explosion of mortgages with multiple risks at the time of issue, like no-money-down loans to people with bad credit histories who didn't verify their incomes. More mortgages and more people taking risks, he said, meant higher home prices and even more speculative activity.

Ackman accused Wall Street of fueling the binge by turning risky mortgages into seemingly safe securities, and turning risky securities into seemingly safe CDOs. CDOs weren't just a bad investment, Ackman contended. They were the linchpin to the mortgage market. In buying up the riskiest tranches of subprime bonds, CDOs made it easier for Wall Street firms to sell their mortgage pools and ultimately the subprime loans themselves. The problem, he warned, was that most of the participants had much more incentive to keep the deals moving than to analyze the risk accurately. "Everybody is getting paid up front, including the rating agencies, except for the ultimate holder of risk," Ackman said.

The danger was that the whole process would abruptly reverse direction if investors began to think they had been had—as they were already beginning to feel.

8

OVER THE CLIFF

It was August 2006. Patty and I had no idea how close our hocus-pocus refinancing scheme had come to blowing apart before we could execute it. And unfortunately, we had no idea that an even bigger calamity was mere days away.

Unbeknownst to us, the subprime business had suffered its first serious cracks by the spring of 2006. Delinquency and foreclosure rates on subprime loans were still low by historical standards, but they were suddenly running higher than normal, accompanied by an ominous new trend: a sudden spike in "early payment defaults." In these cases, borrowers missed payments within the first three months after getting a mortgage. Many of them didn't even bother making a first payment.

In the upside-down logic of the housing bubble, this kind of behavior made perfect sense. These weren't people who had bought expensive houses and immediately felt buyer's remorse. They were

flippers who had bought houses or condos, usually just as construction was starting, and had planned to resell them for a quick profit
as soon as they were completed. In hot markets like Miami and
Fort Lauderdale, you could pull off the whole deal almost without using any of your own money, and sometimes book your profit
before construction was even completed.

By mid-2006, however, prices in many of the hot markets
had suddenly flattened out. Almost overnight, flippers suddenly
couldn't flip. If your only goal had been to resell the property
for a quick gain, making the monthly payments was like throwing good money after bad. In Florida, condo buyers in Miami,
Boca Raton, and countless smaller towns were walking away in
droves.

At Fremont, Kyle Walker had started to choke on early payment
defaults even before Patty and I applied to refinance our loan. As
a rule, investors usually demanded a money-back guarantee on any
loans that defaulted in less than three months. Even though Fremont sold off its mortgages as fast as it could, the company had
already been forced to swallow $238 million in bad loans between
March and June, and the numbers were still climbing.

Less than three weeks after we signed the papers on our mortgage refinance in late June, Fremont announced that it would
stop making even fully documented loans to people with credit
scores below 600. Had we started the process a month or two later,
we wouldn't have made the cut. Patty and I didn't care. We had
bought ourselves breathing room, and we had a plausible plan for
stabilizing our finances. We were still loaded with debt, but we
weren't paying any of those 27 percent interest rates on our credit
cards. Patty was earning a solid salary with a good employer, and
I was earning extra money working overtime at the *Times*. If we
were careful, not only could we meet our monthly expenses, but

we could chip away at our debt and even go out to dinner once in a while.

Both of us were relieved to feel a return to normalcy. Since Patty and I worked within a few blocks of each other and she had a parking space in her building, we drove in to work together most mornings. She would read stories to me from the *Times* and the *Post,* and our conversations blossomed from there. We enjoyed each other's company so much that we never turned on the radio. We had stopped fighting, or even quarreling. We watched TV and read in the evenings before we went to bed, and we even read three of Patty's most beloved books—*The Great Gatsby, To Kill a Mockingbird,* and *The Scarlet Letter*—out loud to each other.

Patty was a muse for me. She prompted me to think in fresh ways about the stories I was covering, and I found myself asking more offbeat questions with her in mind. In fact, I had stumbled into one of my biggest stories in years—a scandal at the Interior Department, which was letting oil companies pump billions of dollars' worth of oil and gas from federal territories without collecting royalties—precisely by asking myself a question that I thought Patty would have asked me about giveaways to the oil industry.

Our brief interlude of optimism and peace ended on October 10, 2006. I was about to learn how sheltered I had been all my life and how unprepared I was for a crisis. I would also learn just how little I understood about either Patty or even myself.

Patty called me at my office shortly before noon. Caller ID showed that she was calling from home, which was odd because we had driven to work together just a few hours earlier.

"I have some bad news," she said.

"You've been fired," I said on impulse, hoping I was wrong.

"Oh my God! Did someone tell you? How did you know?"

I felt the blood drain out of my face as I hunched over my desk and cradled the receiver against my ear.

"It was just a guess," I assured her. "But what the hell happened? I can't believe this." I could feel the clamminess of cold sweat under my shirt. I had a vision of myself falling into an abyss, that I had no moorings and no chance of saving myself. It was good we were talking on the phone. The last thing Patty needed was to see me turn to jelly in front of her.

Patty recounted the story as steadily as she could. Her boss had escorted her to the human resources director after the morning staff meeting. There, as the director stood by to head off any hysterics, her boss told Patty she was being fired. They had already hired a former editor at the *Baltimore Sun* to replace her. If Patty agreed to tell people she was quitting voluntarily—she was well liked, and they didn't want to hurt morale—she would be able to draw her salary for the rest of the month.

"I should have seen it coming," Patty said. "I could tell that she didn't like me. But I couldn't talk to her, or get her to talk to me. I was never able to get her to tell me what the hell she wanted. The only time she spoke to me was when she had something to criticize."

Patty's boss had prepared a list of justifications: Patty had failed to catch proofreading mistakes on this date and that date; she had been past deadline once with the group's weekly online newsletter. There was no mention of how hard she had worked, or how many times she had saved people from their blunders. But the truth was, Patty felt her fate at Pew had been decided early on. Her boss would not tell her what she wanted—would barely talk to her at all, in fact—and gave Patty no chance to make a contribution. There was nothing she could do, though she tried mightily to break through. (It would be cold comfort that the editor who replaced her left the center a year later.)

"Don't worry," she said bravely. "This will not be like the first time I was looking for a job. I've learned so much since then, and I am going to find another job quickly." In the meantime, she said, she could collect unemployment for six months. She would also cash out her retirement account, which had about $7,000 in it.

I wanted to throw up. We had no idea how long it would take for her to find comparable work—or if she even could. I didn't blame Patty for losing her job. I had seen how hard she worked and I knew her skills. She wrote like an angel, she was meticulous, and she knew far more about copyediting than I ever would. I was furious at any boss who would dismiss a person who was capable and hardworking without first trying to smooth out the rough edges.

Yet I failed my first test for supporting her. I should have gone home immediately, but I was so distraught and disoriented that I stayed at work the whole day. I had abandoned Patty in one of her bleakest moments. When I did get home that night, she looked as if she had been crying a good part of the day.

"They had it all planned out," she said morosely. "She was just waiting until she had hired someone else. She decided two weeks into it that I wasn't the kind of person she had thought I was. She thought I was superficial or frivolous. She wanted someone with an impressive résumé, like that guy from the *Sun*."

"She's a moron," I said. I was outraged, because I had seen how dedicated Patty was and how much she often worried about work. "She hired you, and you never pretended to be anything that you weren't," I said. "If she didn't like the way you did things, it was her job to be clear about what she wanted. It seems to me that a good manager has to invest some time and energy in a new employee."

Patty was wracked with guilt over what her being fired would mean for our financial and personal life, but she was also traumatized. For months she had been anxious about work, terrified of letting the slightest typo slip by or of writing something in a style that her boss didn't like. She had taken work home with her, sometimes getting up before dawn to put in extra time. Even so, everything about the office had seemed unfamiliar.

"Here I am, fifty years old, and I hadn't worked as an editor for so long," she said. "Everybody around me was younger. I was coming out of nothingness. I didn't have any prior jobs. I didn't understand workplace politics. I'm a mess."

By any measure, the loss of Patty's job was a financial catastrophe. Between the two of us, we had been bringing home about $6,000 a month—almost $7,500 if you averaged in the twice-a-year payouts I received for overtime. With a monthly mortgage of almost $3,300, two children in the house full-time and three more in the house part-time, it was hard to keep our total expenses below $6,000. The grocery bills alone often totaled close to a thousand bucks. Heating, electricity, water, telephone, Internet, and cable TV could hit another thousand. And those were just the fixed expenses. Without Patty's salary, we would be short at least $3,000 a month.

Cashing in Patty's 401(k) plan would replace her take-home pay for about six weeks. In a testament to her editing skills, a senior researcher who was leaving Pew had asked her to clean up a three-volume book project he had written for Oxford University Press. That would earn her another $5,000. On top of that, she could receive $1,200 a month in unemployment benefits for up to six months. That wouldn't be enough. It was time to bite the bullet and be a real man.

"Hello, Mom?" I said on the phone. "I need to talk to you. Can I come over?"

Even though she was seventy-two years old and only five feet tall, Margaret Andrews Burns could be a force of nature. She had reddish blonde hair, a sweet smile, and an iron will. She had spent the first part of her adult life as a stay-at-home mom and the wife of a diplomat (OK, wife of a CIA operative who was posing as a diplomat). When my father died of a heart attack in 1979, she had become a widow at the age of forty-eight.

My mother had done well for herself. After my father died, she talked her way into a clerical job at the CIA and had gradually worked her way into its professional ranks. Even though her only job in the previous twenty years had been as a part-time salesperson at Garfinkel's department store, she had ended up coordinating training programs for up-and-coming spies. By the time she retired at the age of sixty-five, my mother had put my three younger brothers through college, remodeled the house, and gotten remarried.

Her new husband, Willard Burns, was an elegant but curmudgeonly doctor who had just retired from the Veterans Administration. Willard disapproved of me for all kinds of reasons—he thought I was too liberal, too disorganized, too lax with my children. I was pretty sure he disapproved of my divorce, though he seemed to like Patty. I didn't take it personally, because Willard seemed to disapprove of most people, including my more buttoned-down brothers and their spouses.

"Willard will be playing golf tomorrow morning," my mother suggested pragmatically. "Why don't you come over then?"

Patty was horrified. She hated the idea of borrowing money from anybody, but in particular from my mother. My mother had been polite but chilly toward Patty, and she still maintained close ties with my ex-wife. I didn't care about impressions. I just wanted some money. My grandmother had left a small inheritance for my father, part of which had been reserved for my brothers and me. We were each supposed to get about $60,000. But because of a quirk in the will, my mother had authority over managing the money, even though she wasn't allowed to spend it. I decided it was time to borrow against it.

"Remember how horrible it was when you started to work at the agency, and the people treated you like you couldn't do anything right? You were starting there at the same age Patty is now. Remember how you had that boss who made your life miserable? That's what it's like for Patty."

My mother remembered all too well. She had lived on three continents, learned multiple languages, and socialized with ambassadors and generals. It had been no fun to start out in middle age at the bottom of the career ladder. But her face was grim. "I want to help, but I don't like it," she said wearily. "How much do you think you need?"

I asked for $15,000, which she could take out of my inheritance. I didn't know how long it would take for Patty to get back on her feet. My mother sighed, but she wrote me a check.

Despite this cash infusion, tensions escalated quickly between Patty and me. By Thanksgiving weekend, it had been a month since her last day of work and I was anxious about the job hunt. I knew I shouldn't pressure her, but I was as dependent on her as she was on me.

"So," I said, trying to sound casual. "How goes the job search?"

"There's no point in calling up people right now," she answered curtly. "Nobody makes any hiring decisions going into the Christmas holidays. I can't really find work until January."

"JANUARY?" I erupted. "What the hell do you mean, JANUARY? Even if people aren't hiring right now, that doesn't mean you shouldn't be making contacts and finding out what's going on. You should be calling people up and meeting them. Why wait until they are actually hiring?"

What I really wanted to do was shake her and unleash all the rage, panic, and flawless advice I had been bottling up: *Can't you see we're in a fucking crisis? Why do you keep saying you're doing everything that you possibly can, when all I see is you postponing and making excuses? Show me some panic, because I don't fucking believe you. Get off your ass, get on the telephone, knock on some motherfucking doors.*

"I can't talk to you when you get like this," she said. "I know what I'm doing, and you have to let me do this my way."

Almost instantly, we were in a full-fledged fight. It was an old script, one we had acted out countless times and kept rehearsing and polishing in our heads.

"Why are you treating me like the enemy? Can't you see I'm on your side?" I retorted.

"You're not trying to help me. You're destroying me with your constant nagging and criticism. You never stop. You can never leave it alone. I'm going upstairs."

Following our typical pattern, she ran up to the bedroom, and I followed right behind, getting angrier as I went.

"I have put everything I have on the line for you," I yelled. "I'm the one person who has stuck by you. I'm the one who came up with $15,000, not to mention the money for the house and the $50,000 to clear our credit cards. I've been carrying you for months."

"I knew you would resort to this! You always pick up the closest thing you can to beat me with. You really are a monster. I've got to get out of here. I've made the biggest mistake of my life. Oh my God, why did I ever come here? It would have been so much better if I had just stayed by myself. I could have found a tiny little apartment with Emily."

"Please Patty, listen to me . . ."

"Leave me alone. Leave me the fuck alone! Get out."

As proud as she looked, and as fiery as she could be, her confidence had left her. After twenty years she had jumped into the job market in a new city, and now she had been slapped down and humiliated. Worst of all, she was married to a man who seemed to think she was an idiot. Patty herself didn't entirely understand all her fears at that point. What she did know was that the prospect of job hunting or "networking" made her ill. Over time, in calm moments between fights, she would open up about her misery.

"I always feel like I'm begging for charity," she said. "I feel like all I'm saying is, 'please give me this job.' You have to go in there and act as if you are totally confident. Everybody else knows all these rules about how to act, but I don't. I hate all the game playing and the office politics. It's so fake."

I didn't see the problem. Washington had armies of people who made money by crafting words, organizing presentations, and articulating policy and political issues. I was certain Patty could find a spot for herself in that world. I could visualize it so easily: this intelligent, charming woman chatting up reporters and heavyweight speakers at the start of some think tank conference. She would bring people together, get them talking, and create a little excitement and buzz. But Patty couldn't even imagine that I had such fantasies. She felt lost and belittled, especially by me.

"You're disappointed in me," she would say. "You're trying to make me into somebody I'm not. Maybe you should have stayed married to your ex-wife."

Money and job hunting soon became subjects too explosive to discuss but too crucial to postpone. Patty was feeling more desperate and depressed. The things she did best—being a mother, a partner, a wife, and a lover—didn't seem to be worth much to me. I was trying to be loving and supportive, but my anxiety was as obvious as perspiration. We were at an impasse.

9

ENABLERS OF DISASTER

I f you wanted to mark the exact date when subprime mortgages began to wreck the whole financial system, it would
be July 10, 2007, the day that Moody's Investors Service and
Standard & Poor's tacitly admitted they had blown it. In separate
announcements, the world's two most powerful arbiters of credit
quality slashed their ratings on hundreds of securities backed by
subprime mortgages.

S&P took the ax to 612 different bond issues with a face value
of $8.3 billion. Moody's did the same to 399 securities worth $5.2
billion. Never before had the agencies downgraded so many bonds
at one time, many of them by several steps at once.

Even though the downgrades affected less than 1 percent of the
securities backed by junk mortgages, they still set off a chain reac-
tion that quickly spread around the world. If Moody's and S&P had
bungled the ratings on $13 billion worth of those securities, what

about the other $1.2 trillion in securities that investors were hold-
ing? What about the $1 trillion backed by Alt-A loans? What about
the giant bond insurers who were on the hook in case of defaults?
Who was exposed?

If the agencies had been honest, they might have admitted that
they had grossly understated the dangers of exotic mortgages.
They might have apologized for being at best blind and at worst
corrupt, and confessed that they had no real clue about the safety
of hundreds of billions of dollars' worth of subprime-backed securities that they had branded "triple-A." They might have warned
that the downgrades that day were only the beginning. Maybe they
could have even announced internal investigations, noting that
their blunders had been so egregious that it was hard to believe
they hadn't been intentional.

But no. In a conference call with bond managers and analysts on
July 12 to explain the downgrades, top executives from S&P talked
about their "revised" and "improved" methodologies. At Moody's,
executives droned on about how their downgrades weren't shocking to people who understood how Moody's did its job.

"As most of you know, judging the relative credit risk of securities is not a onetime determination but an ongoing process," said
Richard Cantor, Moody's director of credit policy research. "Right
now we are experiencing unusual market conditions, and if our
ratings did not change to reflect those changing conditions, they
would not be very effective." Translation: don't blame us because
the markets went haywire.

Cantor acknowledged that the number and magnitude of simul-
taneous downgrades had "no precedent" and had "understandably
surprised" people—especially those "who were more familiar with
corporate ratings than with structured finance." Translation: if you

guys actually knew much about mortgage-backed securities, you wouldn't be so surprised.

When one analyst asked if the other securities that Moody's had *not* downgraded were still "OK," another executive tersely answered, "No, the ratings are what they are as of today." Translation: we stand by our ratings—until we change them.

Not surprisingly, the fund managers on that conference call weren't so sanguine. "You had reams upon reams of data about the underwriting of these loans, from the FICO scores to the loan-to-value ratios," said Steven Eisman, a hedge fund manager at Front-Point Partners in Greenwich, Connecticut. "And yet despite all of this data, your original predictions about the potential ranges of performance of the 2006 pools have proven to be completely and utterly wrong. . . . Why do you think you were so off?"

Eisman was just getting started. Why had Moody's and S&P downgraded less than 1 percent of the subprime securities that they had rated? Why should anyone trust their other ratings?

"I have analyzed the data too," Eisman continued, as the Moody's executives listened stonily. "And frankly there are very few pools out there in 2006 that are performing within expectations. The overwhelming majority of 2006 pools are showing delinquency levels [that are] multiples higher than your original assumptions and will certainly generate losses multiples higher than your range would indicate."

It was unusual to vent like that on a conference call, but Eisman was furious. "Help me understand," he said with mocking deference, "why you were downgrading only these bonds when there are thousands that are either as bad or only slightly better?"

The Moody's executives gave long-winded explanations that explained nothing. "What we do when we provide a rating is assess all the information that is available at the time," said Nicholas Weill, the chief credit officer for asset finance. "As we see information evolving, whether we see trends on the performance or we get a better understanding on the origination practices and the servicing practices, we update the ratings as we see fit. And this is what we have been doing since November '06. Operator, next question."

Investors didn't really care what the Moody's executives said. They reacted as if someone had just yelled "FIRE!" in a crowded theater. The Dow Jones Industrial Average dropped 178 points that day as investors bailed out of financial stocks. Money for new subprime mortgages and Alt-A mortgages dried up almost immediately. Soon, money became scarce for all kinds of mortgages, and then for debt that had nothing to do with housing at all.

About 80 percent of the subprime paper was triple-A, which meant it was "good" enough to be in pension funds, money market funds, and all kinds of "conduits" and "structured investment vehicles"—a.k.a. SIVs—that banks had set up for investors. The SIVs and conduits were like robotic investment funds, containers holding big volumes of mortgage-backed securities and other seemingly routine commercial debt. They were part of the plumbing of the financial system, normally invisible. Now they were yet another example of how clogged the financial pipelines had become as a result of junk mortgages. Most of the SIVs were technically kept off banks' balance sheets, meaning that the banks had no financial obligation to protect the SIV investors. But the robots had to be refinanced every three to six months, and suddenly nobody wanted to invest in them. That left the existing SIV investors stuck with billions upon billions' worth of obscure securities that nobody wanted to buy. Banks like Citigroup, the biggest SIV spinner of them all, were forced to buy many of them back.

Fed officials had estimated in August 2006 that about $1 trillion of commercial debt had to be refinanced over the next ninety days. If there weren't any takers, banks like Citigroup would have to either buy back a lot of subprime securities or force their SIV investors to sell them at a big loss.

It began to dawn on people in credit markets around the world that no one really knew how big the losses might be or where they would occur. Who owned those securities? Who had sold them and guaranteed to buy them back? Who had insured them? If you were a bank conducting any kind of financial transaction, whom could you trust? Anybody and everybody was potentially exposed.

As if anybody wanted any more reasons to doubt the rating agencies' credibility, Moody's published a report on July 25, 2007, two weeks after the initial downgrades, assuring people that the financial turmoil had been a "false alarm" and not the start of a real financial collapse. In a breezy, cocky, and amazingly bad assessment, a team of analysts in New York and London told investors to relax.

"Are we one step closer to a financial meltdown?" the Moody's team asked rhetorically. No, it declared. The ability of the big global banks to absorb shocks was "high, perhaps higher than ever." The strength of the core financial institutions was "strong, perhaps stronger than ever." And the markets were still awash with "ample liquidity"—lots of cash. "There is limited risk of market 'seize up' in the current macroeconomic and financial environment," the rating agency predicted.

Oops.

Within three weeks, it was clear that the Big One had arrived. What Moody's had brushed off as a "false alarm" had been the early tremors of a financial collapse that took down much of Wall Street and a big chunk of the economy with it. By the first week in

August 2007, the "ample liquidity" had evaporated and the "seize-up" in credit markets had begun. By the second week in August, banks were afraid to lend to each other. Investors were afraid to refinance short-term commercial debt—even routine corporate IOUs that had nothing to do with mortgages. By the third week, the plutocrats of the modern era—the hedge funds and private equity firms—were getting squeezed.

At the Fed, policy makers had stoically refused to lower interest rates at their meeting on August 7. When the markets kept crashing, they dropped their pose of cool detachment and hit the panic button. On August 17, the Fed announced a dramatic expansion of its emergency loan program for banks and all but promised to flood the markets with cheap money.

"Financial market conditions have deteriorated," the central bank said in one of its characteristically anodyne announcements. It warned that tightening credit and rising uncertainty had "the potential to restrain growth going forward." As a result, the "downside risks to economic growth have increased appreciably." The money sentence was that policy makers were "prepared to act as needed" if things got worse.

In Fedspeak, the message to Wall Street, loosely translated, was "ALL RIGHT, ALREADY! We get it! We really, truly understand that we could have a disaster on our hands. But trust us. We will do whatever it takes to prevent it."

The crisis was official, and the mother of all bailouts had begun.

By darkly poetic coincidence, each of my own mortgage lenders had a direct link to the events of July 10, 2007. It turned out that Fremont Investment & Loan had been a leading cause of Moody's downgrades that day. American Home Mortgage, meanwhile, collapsed three weeks after the announcement. My third lender, JPMorgan Chase, emerged as a huge winner from the wreckage.

It was a perverse variation on what the economist Joseph Schumpeter called "creative destruction." Schumpeter argued that capitalism was a constant and often brutal clash between the old and the new, the good and the better. Companies and industries were constantly replaced and reborn. The mortgage meltdown, by contrast, was more like creative self-destruction. The greediest and most reckless institutions were destroying themselves and being taken over or replaced by the ones that had been slightly less greedy and reckless.

According to Moody's, Fremont Investment & Loan was right at the center of the rating agency's bombshell announcement on July 10. Moody's said that 63 percent of the securities it downgraded that day had been backed by mortgages from only four lenders. Fremont was at the very top of the short list, accounting for 19 percent of the downgrades. It was followed by three of its neighbors down in Orange County: New Century Financial, which had gone bankrupt in April; Long Beach Mortgage, owned by Washington Mutual; and WMC Mortgage, owned by General Electric. As rough-and-tumble as Fremont was, I was startled to see it playing such a prominent role as a catalyst for the broader meltdown. Fremont was smaller than Countrywide, less visible than New Century, and less sleazy than some of the real bucket shops.

But why had Moody's waited so long to act? The Federal Deposit Insurance Corporation had already forced Fremont out of the subprime business back in March. Its management had been replaced in June. New Century had gone bankrupt and shut its doors in February, in what would be the biggest corporate bankruptcy of 2007. Scores of smaller subprime lenders had either gone out of business or had become zombie companies—living, but dead.

Back on the East Coast, Michael Strauss and American Home Mortgage became immediate victims of the panic. Within days of the ratings announcement, Strauss's credit lines became prohibitively expensive. It was like being cut off from oxygen. The company couldn't close on new mortgages because it couldn't deliver the cash to its borrowers. The real problem, of course, was American Home's $15 billion leveraged portfolio of high-risk mortgages. Those mortgages and mortgage-backed securities had plunged in value. Strauss's creditors were all demanding that he put up more cash to make up for the declining value of his collateral. Strauss didn't have that kind of money. By August 2, faster than he ever dreamed possible, American Home Mortgage was out of business and in bankruptcy court.

My third lender, JPMorgan Chase, would become one of the few victorious survivors of the crisis. The company had not been shy about either making junk mortgages or bundling them into securities; but unlike Merrill Lynch or Citigroup, it had been careful to resell them and get them off its own books. Because JPMorgan Chase was one of the few big banks that wasn't imploding, the Federal Reserve relied on it in March 2008 to take over Bear Stearns, the fourth biggest investment bank on Wall Street.

Bear Stearns had been one of Wall Street's most experienced players in the mortgage market. Its rivals had envied Bear's end-to-end mortgage machine, which included a major subprime mortgage lender, a "servicing" company that collected payments and took care of customers, and of course a securitization factory to bundle and resell all those loans for a profit. But Bear was caught holding its own troubled assets, and its stock came under brutal attack from short-sellers who insisted it was insolvent. By March, institutional customers were pulling their money out of Bear, creating the equivalent of a modern-day run on the bank. Almost overnight, Bear found itself literally insolvent. To prevent Bear from going bankrupt and unleashing chaos on Wall Street, the Fed loaned JPMorgan Chase $29 billion to acquire Bear and make good on its obligations.

It was hard to believe that Moody's, Standard & Poor's, and Fitch Ratings could unleash so much chaos. In some ways, it was hard to believe how slavishly bond managers picked securities solely on the basis of how many A's, B's, and C's a security had been given. It was as if the world's big institutional funds had outsourced their brains to a call center in Mumbai.

For me, though, as someone who still couldn't believe how much money he had been loaned, the most amazing discovery was how basic and simple the errors of the rating agencies had been. The errors had nothing to do with erroneous tweaks to a vast computer modeling system.

In essence, the agencies had used bogus assumptions to justify absurd conclusions. The bogus assumptions were more than errors; they were rationalizations for judgments that had no basis in fact. The flaws were so basic and so glaring that it was hard to believe they hadn't been intentional. And indeed, a handful of experts had pointed to them long before the subprime market collapsed.

"We got what we deserved," said David Einhorn, the director of Greenlight Capital, in a speech in October 2007. "This crisis wasn't an accident. We didn't get unlucky. This crisis came because there have been a lot of bad practices and bad ideas."

It was easy to be flummoxed by the complex mathematical models that Moody's and S&P used to analyze risk. It was even easier to be intimidated by the rococo intricacies of the securities themselves. As Ben S. Bernanke, the Fed chairman, had himself plaintively remarked in 2007, "I'd just like to know what's in the damn things." For all their sophistication, the rating models were based on data about the past performance of subprime mortgages. That was the most obvious problem: there was no valid data on past performance for the kinds of mortgages that had swept the country after 2003.

Bill Gross, the chief investment officer at PIMCO, the giant bond management firm based in Newport Beach, California, summarized the problem bluntly in a commentary on his website in June 2007: the agencies had been seduced by cheap lipstick and hooker heels. "Our prim remembrance of Gidget going to Hawaii and hanging out with the beach boys seems to have been replaced by an image of Heidi Fleiss setting up a floating brothel in Beverly Hills," Gross wrote. What Gross meant was that the rating agencies, lulled by the money they were earning from the Wall Street mortgage machine, had made the mistake of believing that the razzle-dazzle new mortgages were pretty much the same as older varieties.

Although subprime mortgages had originated in the mid-1990s, they were still a fringe business until about 2001. And what had seemed like high-risk subprime loans in 2000 were tame compared with the ones that came along at the height of the housing bubble. The popular but lethal "pay-option" loans, like "Power ARMs," didn't debut until 2003.

Instead of admitting that both the housing market and the mortgage business had entered uncharted territory, the agencies had acted as if they knew what to expect. Supporters of option ARMs and all the other novel mortgages invariably pointed out that the default rates were remarkably low. But a booming real estate market and a strong economy could do wonders to gloss over credit problems. When fewer people were unemployed, fewer people fell behind on their payments. Rising home prices, meanwhile, gave people a host of escape hatches if they got into trouble. They could refinance a crummy subprime loan with a cheaper conventional one. They could pull cash out of the house with a home equity loan. If all else failed, they could sell the house rather than lose it to foreclosure.

The big question was, what happens during bad times? As recently as 2004, Moody's and S&P both assumed that the losses from a pool of subprime loans would never rise above 5 percent. In 2006, they had raised that loss assumption to 6 percent. As it happened, the loss rate on many pools turned out to be closer to 20 percent.

According to a Moody's report in March 2007, 6 percent was the loss rate for the worst "vintage" of subprime mortgages on record: those made in 2000, just before the recession hit in 2001. Unfortunately, the recession of 2001 was a terrible benchmark for predicting losses in the next downturn. It had been one of the shortest and mildest recessions in decades, and it was one of the very few in which property prices climbed rapidly. As we've seen, we had Alan Greenspan to thank for those property prices.

No one on Wall Street seemed to be troubled by the fact that the unprecedented housing boom over the previous ten years had created a false picture of junk mortgages. I had asked Moody's about this in May 2005, when home prices were still hopping and the living was easy. The company arranged a telephone interview for me with Carlos Maymi, then a vice president and senior credit officer.

What I remember most vividly is that I could barely stay awake, and I suspect this wasn't unusual. Flooding the conversation with complicated, mind-numbing jargon is a great way to satisfy reporters' interview requests without letting them ask probing questions. Maymi droned in a resonant baritone about things like tranches, credit enhancement, and overcollateralization. My head swirled in confusion. Who was I to argue that Moody's wasn't demanding the right amount of collateralization? Maymi confidently explained that Moody's had a system called Moody's Mortgage Metrics, which could simulate the performance of novel mortgages under all kinds of different economic conditions. "We ran 1,200 economic scenarios," Maymi said. "If you buy an MBS [mortgage-backed security], we're confident of the performance through a wide variety of harsh environments."

What mattered, of course, was which scenarios the agencies chose to believe. None of them apparently believed in a scenario in which home prices kept falling, default rates soared, home prices fell some more, and people were too worried about their finances to do much spending at Christmas. As scenarios went, that one was at least as believable as the one that assumed home prices would keep climbing forever.

"The errors were forecastable," said Charles Calomiris, a professor of housing finance at Columbia University's school of business. "In fact, they had been pointed out long before the crash began."

The more you dug into the rating agency's approaches, the more appalling they seemed. The dirty secret was that the flaws hadn't been a secret. Smart bond investors had been trashing subprime-backed securities for almost a year before the agencies started to come clean. The sea change that began on July 10, 2007, wasn't that investors abruptly stopped believing the ratings. The real change seemed to be that investors had to stop *pretending* they believed the ratings.

"What really amazes me about this was how the smart money made these kinds of mistakes," said Calomiris. "We're not talking about gullible people who had no clue about what was going on. These were very sophisticated institutional investors. You had plenty of signs of a housing bubble by 2005, and by 2006 there wasn't any mistake of it. Yet they stayed in there."

You couldn't blame the media for ignoring the story. Bad news is good news. It's in our DNA. And if ever there had seemed to be a disaster in the making, it was the housing bubble. *The New York Times, Wall Street Journal, Business Week,* and local newspapers like the *Orange County Register* had been publishing scores of scare stories for at least two years. Starting in 2005, the *Times* had assigned at least two reporters to cover the housing bubble full-time. At least a dozen other reporters, including me, were writing about the mounting dangers from the vantage point of our separate beats.

If many people understood that the risks were higher than the rating agencies thought, why were investors shocked by the downgrades?

Moody's and S&P's power stemmed from more than their repu tations. Insurance companies, pension funds, and countless other investors had legal and regulatory obligations to keep some of their holdings in securities rated triple-A or at least "investment grade." If ratings went down, many fund managers had to start dumping their securities, in turn depressing their market value even further than the rating change itself. It was a double whammy.

Yet there was a more disturbing answer. Calomiris, in a paper he delivered at the 2008 Federal Reserve symposium in Jackson Hole, Wyoming, argued that fund managers found it convenient to pretend that the rating agencies knew what they were talking about. "Investors could have balked," Calomiris noted. "Why didn't they? Because they were investing someone else's money and earning huge salaries, bonuses, and management fees for being willing to pretend that these were reasonable investments."

"They knew they would be able to blame the collapse, when it inevitably came, on a surprising shock," Calomiris said. "The script would be clear and would give 'plausible deniability' to all involved: 'Who knew? We all thought that six percent was the right loss assumption! That was what experience suggested and what the rating agencies used.'"

The conspiracy of silence couldn't go on forever. Smart investors had been quietly short-selling the subprime mortgage market long before the rating agencies grudgingly came clean. You had to be blind not to see the trouble mounting. In May 2007, Bear Stearns admitted that it was having problems with two hedge funds that had loaded up on subprime mortgage-backed securities. It was all supposed to be triple-A–rated securities, but that wasn't much comfort. A lot of those securities were CDOs, the raunch-tranche garbage collectors of the securitization world. Both funds had bought some of their securities "on margin," which is to say they had borrowed part of the money to pay for their securities. As investor anxiety about subprime defaults escalated, the market value of the funds' holdings had fallen and they had to meet margin calls from creditors. In June, Bear Stearns was forced to inject $3.2 billion into the funds to keep them afloat.

It was hard to overstate the importance of Moody's, S&P, and Fitch Ratings, the third big rating agency. In business for nearly a century, they were supposed to be the definitive authorities on evaluating credit risk. With armies of analysts, elaborate mathematical models, and access to confidential data at every organization they rated, the big three had analyzed almost every institution that borrowed money by selling bonds, whether it was Microsoft, the city of Chicago, or Brazil.

In many ways, the agencies were like government regulators. Pension funds, money market funds, and legions of other institutional investors were required by law to keep minimum amounts of their money in securities with triple-A or other high ratings. As the gatekeepers to a financial Holy Grail, the rating agencies' ability to set the requirements for grades like triple-A effectively put them in charge of protecting the public by regulating the safety and soundness of debt securities.

Unlike a government agency, the rating companies were for-profit companies that earned their revenue by selling their rating services to the companies they were supposed to be supervising. Adding to the conflict of interest, the agencies earned their fees only if the Wall Street firm successfully sold the securities they had just rated. The paradox had existed for decades, and there weren't any easy ways to eliminate it.

One thing was clear: the agencies had been making excellent profits from the subprime boom. Moody's, a publicly traded company, saw its revenues double from $1.02 billion in 2002 to $2.2 billion in 2007. Its operating profit hovered around a very plush 50 percent of revenues throughout that period.

David Einhorn, the founder of Greenlight Capital, made a strong case that the agencies' best customers—the Wall Street firms and the bond insurers—had corrupted them. Thin and boyish, Einhorn looked as if he was still in his twenties. He had already become legendary as an activist investor who had profited mightily by shorting companies that manipulated their earnings.

Einhorn added to his reputation as a wunderkind by taking part in the 2006 World Series of Poker in Las Vegas. At the time, he said, he had almost no experience with Texas hold 'em. That didn't stop him from staying in the game until it was down to the last two tables. Einhorn walked away with $659,730—which he donated to the Michael J. Fox Foundation for Parkinson's Research.

Einhorn had been burned by mortgage lenders. He had been an investor in both American Home Mortgage and New Century Financial. Both investments had gone sour. Still, he reserved special venom for the rating agencies. "If you read Moody's investor presentation, you will see that the reason to buy Moody's stock is to participate in the growth of structured finance," Einhorn said in a speech he gave to investors in October 2007. "Moody's business is to support that growth, and Moody's shareholders depend on this."

In a withering analysis, Einhorn then showed that it was easier for a super-risky collateralized debt obligation to get a triple-A rating than it was for a corporate bond to earn that rating, and easier for a corporate bond to get the top rating than for a municipal bond to do so. Specifically, he said, the average triple-A–rated municipal bond had a lower default rate than the average triple-A–rated corporate bond, which in turn had a lower default rate than that of the average mortgage-backed CDO.

Cities and towns across the country were being overcharged, Einhorn argued, while Wall Street firms were getting their clients a good deal. "The agencies can't risk alienating them," Einhorn said. "If Pocatello, Idaho, doesn't like its rating, it has no leverage with Fitch. Wall Street is a different story."

As the full horror of the financial mess became apparent, people at Moody's and Standard & Poor's began to show remorse. "We drank the Kool-Aid," admitted Ray McDaniel, chief executive of Moody's, in a presentation for company executives in late 2007, which was later made public by the House Committee on Oversight and Government Reform.

"It turns out that ratings quality has surprisingly few friends," McDaniels continued. "Issuers want high ratings; investors don't want ratings downgrades; short-sighted bankers labor short-sightedly to game the ratings agencies."

10

BULL IN THE SUBPRIME SHOP

When I first talked to Bill Dallas in June 2004, he was one of the few go-go lenders in southern California who was appalled by the housing boom and cheap money. "Lending standards have loosened to historic levels," he complained. "Nobody is heeding the yield signs." There were too many amateur lenders, too many dumb ideas and too many borrowers being encouraged to lie. As Milton Friedman might have said, there was too much money chasing too few decent borrowers.

"This is what always happens at the end of a cycle," Dallas told me while I was working on a story about the explosion in easy mortgages. "Everybody jumps into the business because they see all the money being made. Then the underwriting standards get loosened, because of all the competition. The problem is that most people have only been in the business for a few years and have never experienced a down market."

Dallas wasn't a prude about racy mortgages. With his blue eyes, crew-cut gray hair, trim physique, and year-round tan, he was a charter member of southern California's exotic lending scene. His first company, First Franklin Financial Corporation, pioneered some of the first no-money-down mortgages and evolved into a major subprime lender. His newest venture, Ownit Mortgage Solutions in Agoura Hills, California, was a fast-growing start-up that quintupled its loan volume in 2004 to $4 billion.

Thanks largely to exotic mortgages, Dallas and the good life had been acquainted for a long time. He lived in a majestic Georgian mansion in the gated community of Lake Sherwood, about twenty miles inland from Malibu. Angelo Mozilo of Countrywide Financial lived just a few blocks away. As a sideline, Dallas managed the financial empire of Mary-Kate and Ashley Olsen, the Olsen twins.

Given his early warnings about reckless lending, it came as a shock when Dallas became one of the first casualties of . . . reckless lending. On December 7, 2006, Ownit Mortgage Solutions filed for bankruptcy, and Dallas dismissed virtually all of its more than eight hundred employees. A shocking number of Ownit's mortgages had either defaulted within their first few months or been "kicked out" of investment pools because of deficiencies in their underwriting. Dallas had already been forced to buy back $500 million worth of mortgages, which he could sell only at a big loss, and his biggest buyers were screaming for him to take back $165 million more. Some of the loudest screams came from Ownit's biggest buyer and creditor, Merrill Lynch, which was also one of Ownit's biggest shareholders.

In an interview with Vikas Bajaj of *The New York Times* not long after he shut down the company, Dallas complained that Merrill Lynch had pressured him to lower his standards in order to keep up his loan production. When the defaults started to pile up, Dallas complained, Merrill Lynch not only left him stranded but started canceling his credit lines. Dallas's complaint—despite the devil-made-me-do-it overtones—had the ring of truth. I wanted to dig deeper.

If I had learned one thing from the odyssey of Fremont's junk loans, it was how ravenous Wall Street had been to buy them. No matter how reckless the subprime lender was, its money had come from Wall Street's insatiable securitization mills. Goldman Sachs, JPMorgan Chase, Lehman Brothers, and almost every other big firm—not to mention countless hedge funds and boutique investment shops—had been falling over themselves to buy whatever dreck Fremont had to offer.

Merrill Lynch had been so hungry for junk loans that it paid $100 million in September 2005 for a one-fifth stake in Ownit. That translated to a valuation of $500 million, a rich price for a two-year-old business with few assets and huge competitors. Dallas and his partners had invested only $38 million when they opened the shop. As part of the deal, Ownit agreed to sell Merrill at least two-thirds of the mortgages it made. Merrill became one of Ownit's biggest sources of "warehouse" credit, the short-term financing that lenders use to pay for mortgages before selling them to investors.

There wasn't any mystery to what Merrill wanted from Ownit: a captive junk loan supplier to feed its own end-to-end subprime money machine. Fannie Mae and Freddie Mac had a lock on bundling traditional conforming loans, and those offered much less profit anyway. By 2005, subprime and Alt-A loans were as big a business as conforming loans, and profit margins were much higher.

Under E. Stanley O'Neal, Merrill had gone from being an also-ran in mortgage-backed securities to a top-ranked player. Thanks to Christopher Ricciardi, later of Libertas III fame, Merrill was the number one producer of collateralized debt obligations. Between mortgage-backed bonds, CDOs, and credit-default swaps on all those securities, junk mortgages had become Merrill's biggest source of growth. Merrill's pretax profits in 2005 soared 27 percent to a new record of $7.4 billion, and they climbed another 40 percent in 2006, to $10.4 billion. Profit margins widened to new records too, hitting 30.1 percent in 2006.

But Merrill Lynch wasn't content with its stake in Ownit. In an amazing display of hubris, Merrill proudly announced in September 2006 that it was paying $1.3 billion for First Franklin Financial, Dallas's first company, which he had sold for a fraction of that price to National City Bank. By this time the great housing boom was already ending, the cracks in the subprime industry had started to spread, and almost all those who had designed subprime mortgages knew they were headed for huge problems as soon as housing prices stopped climbing and people couldn't refinance. When the First Franklin deal closed in January, dozens of subprime lenders were already either shutting down or scaling back.

Merrill wasn't alone. Many on Wall Street envied Lehman Brothers and Bear Stearns, both of which had bought subprime shops years earlier. In December 2006, Morgan Stanley had plunked down $706 million for a subprime lender called Saxon Capital. Deutsche Bank, the giant German bank known for its stodginess, had bought a big Alt-A lender called MortgageIT in 2005. By August 2007, the whole business would be dead.

I decided to visit Bill Dallas in June 2008, while I was in California to research the mortgage companies' role in my own debacle. Dallas had not been one of my lenders, but he had been part of my early education in go-go mortgages. He had also been at the nexus between the subprime pioneers in Orange County and the securitizers on Wall Street.

At first, Dallas begged off. He was sick of the whole subject and he felt bruised. He knew that *subprime* had become a synonym for sleazy, reckless, and fraudulent, and he hated being lumped in with the debacle. On a personal level, he had been forced to lay off all the people he had recruited away from other jobs. Some of those people were still bitter toward him.

Eventually, he relented. I found him in a humble set of offices on the second story of a strip shopping center in the wealthy town of Westlake Village, California. The offices were sunny and over-looked Lake Sherwood, but they hardly looked like the base for a multimillionaire who still had a slew of business ventures. Dallas didn't care. He had picked the location because it was five minutes from his home. His one assistant, Angel, answered the phones and handled administrative chores.

Dallas greeted me in khaki slacks and a blue golf shirt. Like many California financial types, he had a way of looking both utterly casual and ready to pounce on a deal at a moment's notice. At the time I arrived, he had been watching a replay of his son's Little League game on a wide-screen TV in his office. Westlake Village was the kind of place where local Little League games were routinely carried on public-access cable channels.

I had assumed that anybody who loaned money to creepy peo-ple was probably a creep too, but Dallas seemed like a happy warrior who loved what he did. He could talk for hours about how the business had evolved, why southern California was its epicen-ter, and what its financial underpinnings were. In some ways, he was an oddball for southern California. Raised in Ohio, he had graduated from Bowling Green University and was still a major contributor to his alma mater. In a region of the country where the dominant religion was conspicuous consumption, Dallas was a deeply religious Christian who had founded the Oaks Christian

School in Westlake Village and was president of the California
Lutheran University.

Dallas saw himself as lending to people who were good credit
risks but didn't fit the Ozzie-and-Harriet profiles that "A" lenders
wanted to see. "You can't make any money by lending inside the
box," he said. "The question is, how do you lend money to people
who are outside the box?"

He had spent years experimenting with mortgages that were
"outside the box," and he seemed convinced that such mortgages,
done properly, could both expand home ownership and be a lucrative investment. He came across as idealistic, not because he
preached about high-minded goals but because of the obvious zeal
he put into figuring out what worked and what didn't.

Dallas thought it was natural and often appropriate for people
to stretch their finances when buying a house. He also thought it
could be appropriate to lend people 100 percent of the purchase
price of a home. He understood that people sometimes had nasty
credit scores because of onetime calamities. "We all know people
who have had credit scores swing from 850 to 450, because life
beats the shit out of you," he remarked.

At the same time, Dallas thought it was madness to take on any
of those risks without reliable information about a person's income,
assets, and honesty. If he was going to bend the traditional rules, he
said, he wanted to know what he was getting into. That made his
approach different from most subprime lenders in several ways.

For starters, he looked for borrowers with decent credit scores—
not necessarily in the "very good" range above 720, but generally
above 660, the informal dividing line between "prime" and "subprime." In 2004, Ownit's first full year of operation, the company's average borrower had had a respectable credit score of 690.
It wasn't Ozzie and Harriet, but it was much higher than the

subprime borrowers at bucket shops like Option One (owned by H&R Block), WMC (General Electric), or Long Beach Mortgage (Washington Mutual).

Unlike his competitors, Dallas insisted on verifying a person's income: pay stubs, tax returns, bank statements, the works. For people who were self-employed and didn't have paychecks, Ownit demanded alternative documentation like bank statements for the previous six months. Up through 2005, Dallas claimed, between 80 and 90 percent of Ownit's mortgages had been based on verified incomes.

By contrast, a typical subprime lender was doing at least half its business in stated-income liar's loans. If lenders ran across information on a person's bank statements that cast doubt on the stated income, many instructed underwriters to scrupulously ignore it. And that was for borrowers who already had scary credit histories or were applying for hinky mortgages like option ARMs.

"The key to our secret sauce was getting all of our income verified," Dallas said. "I say, how are you going to screw me? You're going to lie about your income, lie about your assets, and lie about the value of your house. A broker will commit fraud to get you to qualify."

For the first two years, the formula worked well. Dallas and his financial backers, a private equity firm owned by Bank of America, had created Ownit by taking over a tiny mortgage lender in 2003, renaming it, and then dramatically expanding. He recruited scores of former executives from First Franklin and set up new offices around the country.

"When Bill left First Franklin and started Ownit, roughly half of First Franklin's people followed him out of sheer loyalty," said Robin Medecke, a former manager at First Franklin in Ohio, who is now a blogger for the Mortgage Lender Implode-O-Meter.

Like First Franklin, Ownit was a "wholesale" lender that didn't market directly to home buyers. Instead, its "account executives" marketed through thousands of independent mortgage brokers who brought mortgages to them for approval. Ownit's loan volumes sky-rocketed from $800 million in 2003 to $4 billion in 2004 and $8 billion in 2005. By the time Merrill Lynch invested its $100 million in September 2005, the cheeky startup was making almost $1 billion a month in loans. It was the fastest-growing subprime lender in the country, though admittedly it was growing from a tiny base.

For Brad Cottrell, a former paramedic who became one of Ownit's top salespeople, it was as if trucks filled with money were unloading at his house every other day. An account representative typically earned 40 "basis points," or 0.4 percent, on each loan he or she brought in. Cottrell, who was in his early thirties and mar-ried with two small children, was landing $20 million in new mort-gages a month and earning almost $1 million a year. "Bill became my business idol," he told me. Cottrell loved the work and entre-preneurial excitement that Dallas brought to the young company. "He was an awesome presenter. He would talk and you would just say, 'Yeah, Yeah, Yeah! Let's go!'"

"I bought this gi-normous house in 2005—5,200 square feet, a view of the ocean—and I put $500,000 into improvements to it, like a pool," Cottrell recounted. All told, he put about $2.1 million into the house, and he took out an option ARM mortgage from Countrywide Financial for $1.7 million. The monthly payments were steep, but the housing market was on fire and Cottrell had money to burn.

Even Bill Dallas admitted that what happened next wasn't Mer-rill Lynch's fault. At almost exactly the moment that Merrill was paying $100 million for its stake in Ownit, bond investors suddenly turned against the company's mortgages with a herdlike swiftness.

The problem wasn't that Ownit's mortgages were going sour. At that point, they weren't. The problem was that investors suddenly didn't want to pay a premium for credit quality. They didn't care if Dallas's borrowers had higher credit scores or had documented their incomes. What they wanted was mortgages that paid higher interest rates. The market preferred sleaze over safety.

In the jargon of mortgage trading, Ownit had been selling its loans for as much as "104," which meant that investors would pay as much as 4 percentage points above the combined loan balance. On $1 billion in loans, Ownit would reap an extra $40 million. That was a huge margin, enough for Dallas to cover his operating expenses and still have a fat profit. In October 2006, the market mood changed. Investors didn't like that Ownit's average interest rate was "only" 6.87 percent. Even though that was well above the rate on ordinary conforming mortgages, it was well below the 8.5 or 8.75 percent that banks like New Century and Countrywide were getting on their subprime loans.

"All of a sudden, our business model is no longer successful," Dallas recounted, talking in the present tense as if he were still there. "I am not getting paid for the quality of my credit. Nobody cares about full-doc loans. The market is saying it wants higher coupon rates."

The suddenness of the shift mystified him, but he couldn't do anything about it. With long-term interest rates still at historic lows, investment managers were chasing higher yields. With subprime default rates still remarkably low, they went for dodgier mortgages that paid higher rates. To anyone who added up all the elements, it was crazy: no income verification; borrowers with abysmal credit histories; borrowers with no equity in the house; mortgages with payments that were spring-loaded to jump 30 percent or more after a few years.

Yet as one high-ranking Wall Street executive explained to me long after the bubble had burst, the logic seemed unshakable at the time. "You have to remember that home mortgages have a track record for safety that goes back for a century," this executive said. "People have always paid their mortgages before they paid anything else, and we have data on that going back decades. Second, home prices had never gone down for a full year since at least the end of World War II. From an investment perspective, you can raise capital at 5 percent a year and lend it out at 8 percent or 8.5 percent. There is more risk in those mortgages, but the value of the houses is going up. We don't think many borrowers will actually default. But because the houses are going up in value, you don't face the risk of a big loss even on a house that does go into foreclosure."

"There was almost no risk," he summed up with utter calm. "It was almost like free money."

At Ownit's board meeting in January 2006—with Michael Blum, Merrill Lynch's chief of global structured finance, now a director of the company—Dallas outlined the choice he faced. He could lower his standards, chase the higher mortgage rates, and go for maximum volume. That would boost initial profits and spread his fixed costs over more mortgages, he said, but soaring default rates could come back to haunt them. Or he could try to cut back on loan volumes and sit on the sidelines until lenders regained their sanity.

"They thought we were a bunch of knuckleheads," Dallas said, "They kept saying we were leaving money on the table, that we needed to accept lower FICO scores and do more stated-income loans. They told us they had studied all kinds of data, which showed that stated-income loans didn't add much risk."

"I told them, I have to make a big decision," Dallas said. "Do I try to chase the market and go after the higher coupon rate, or do we get smaller? The answer was, damn the torpedoes and full speed ahead."

Dallas wasn't the only person who was baffled by what investors were doing. The growing lust for higher yields from liar's loans was part of a broader story that was perplexing Alan Greenspan at the Federal Reserve. Greenspan, then in his last year as Fed chairman, couldn't understand why investors had dismissed the Fed's ongoing series of increases in its benchmark interest rate.

Ordinarily, an increase in the so-called federal funds rate—the rate that banks charge for lending each other their reserves—leads to an increase in long-term interest rates for things like home loans. The Fed had been raising the overnight rate since June 2004, and long-term rates and mortgage rates had actually edged down.

Testifying before the Senate Banking Committee in February 2005, Greenspan called it a "conundrum" and didn't sound happy about it. He thought it was high time for the housing market to cool down. Instead, with mortgage rates so stubbornly low, the housing boom was getting hotter and wilder.

Bond investors were getting wilder too. With so much cheap money looking for something to do, Wall Street firms and institutional investors were all desperately looking for ways to bump up their returns. Conservative investors like university endowment funds were plowing money into hedge funds, lightly regulated investment companies that employed arcane strategies and used borrowed money to torque up their returns. Bond funds bid up the prices of "high-yield" corporate junk bonds so much that the "high" yields were only 3 or 4 percentage points above Treasury rates. The availability of so much cheap money from all over the world had made bond investors so desperate for a return—any return—that they were willing to accept amazingly low compensation for comparatively high risk. Wall Street firms like Goldman Sachs were goosing their own returns, running up $38 in debt for every $1 in equity.

The most popular place to ratchet up risk without appearing to do so was the US housing market. It is no coincidence that subprime and Alt-A securitizations tripled from $300 billion in 2002 to $1 trillion in 2006. By contrast, securitizations of "conforming" mortgages by Fannie Mae and Freddie Mac plunged from $1.7 trillion in 2002 to only $1 trillion in 2006.

Greenspan, despite his apparent refusal to address the dangers building up in junk mortgages, uttered his haunting prophecy—"history has not dealt kindly with the aftermath of protracted periods of low risk"—just a few weeks before investors began rejecting Ownit's mortgages as too tame.

It was Ben S. Bernanke, a Fed governor who would succeed Greenspan as Fed chairman, who proposed a catchy and all-too-soothing explanation for both mysteries: a "global savings glut." In a lecture at the St. Louis Fed in March 2005, Bernanke argued that China and other Asian countries were saving so much of the money they reaped from exports that they couldn't find enough to invest in at home. Those pent-up savings had become a "glut," a glob of money totaling hundreds of billions of dollars a year that was pouring into the United States.

In a way, Bernanke was simply putting an unconventional new spin on the much-discussed increase in US foreign indebtedness. It was no secret that the United States was running huge foreign trade deficits and had become the world's biggest debtor nation. Nor was it a secret that China and other Asian countries were financing those deficits by buying staggering amounts of Treasury securities (and, not incidentally, mortgage-backed securities from Fannie Mae and Freddie Mac).

Bernanke made this sound like a good thing. The problem wasn't that Americans saved too little and spent too much, Bernanke suggested. The problem was that other countries were saving too much and didn't have enough investment opportunities at home. The United States, with its rising productivity, "low political risk," and respect for property rights, Bernanke said, had become "exceptionally attractive to international investors." The flood of incoming money, he said, had kept interest rates remarkably low and in turn had fueled record levels of home construction and home sales.

"From a narrow US perspective, these low long-term rates are puzzling," Bernanke said. "From a global perspective, they may be less so."

This seemed to defang the critics who moaned that the United States was a profligate and mismanaged country. Bernanke cautioned that he wasn't making a "value judgment," but his clear implication was that neither the American government nor American shoppers needed to berate themselves about all their borrowing.

Money was cheap, he seemed to be saying. Live with it.

———

For Bill Dallas, the flood of cheap money was a big problem. His entire business model had been based on finding ways to expand the reach of mortgages without running up too much risk. He had boiled down his formula to a mantra that he drilled into everyone who worked for him: owner-occupied homes, no investment properties; single-family homes, no condos; purchase-money, no refinancing; full-doc loans, no liar's loans; and a decent credit history. Neither Michael Blum nor Matthew Whalen, the Merrill executive who controlled Merrill's "warehouse" credit lines, had actually forced Dallas to join the mortgage mayhem, though Dallas didn't think he had much choice.

"My 20 percent owners, who had my credit line, were telling me that you've got to get to a higher coupon rate because if you don't we won't make any money on them," Dallas said. Besides, Merrill was buying two-thirds of Ownit's mortgages. Who else would buy his loans if Merrill didn't? And if they wanted to buy them, why not sell them? The customer was always right.

Immediately, the average credit score of Ownit's new borrowers dropped from 690 to about 630, which was going from comfortably prime to solidly subprime. The share of stated-income loans climbed from almost zero to more than 30 percent. The message to all the independent brokers was that Ownit would not be scrutinizing the paperwork too closely.

The results were infinitely more disastrous than even Dallas had expected. Early payment defaults—borrowers defaulting within the first three months—soared from zero to 3 percent of new mortgages between December 2005 and May 2006. That was a staggering number. As recently as 2004, the foreclosure rate over the entire lifetimes of subprime loans had been less than 3 percent.

Worse yet, Merrill Lynch and other buyers were forcing Ownit to back another big share of its mortgages because of problems like inflated property appraisals. Ownit would then have to try to resell those loans, but they would be branded as defective and would inevitably sell at a big loss. "We went from zero kick-outs in 2005 to almost 10 percent by mid- to late 2006," Dallas said. Ownit had to take back $500 million worth of mortgages, which would be classified as "scratch and dent" loans that could be resold only at a steep loss.

Worst of all, 75 percent of those loans were coming back from

Merrill Lynch, Dallas's supposed partner and the company that had pushed him to go with the flow.

Dallas immediately slammed Ownit into reverse. First he stopped all lending to people with credit scores below 620, then to people with credit scores below 640. By mid-June, he had wiped out all stated-income liar's loans. The early-default rate came back down to 1.5 percent, but Ownit's loan volumes plunged 40 percent, from $1 billion a month to $600 million.

The pattern was strikingly similar to what had happened at Fremont, where Kyle Walker had abruptly clamped down on low credit scores and no-doc loans in June. Other lenders were running into the same thing, and there was a common link: their exposure to loans in Miami, Palm Beach, and other parts of South Florida. Miami's condo market had been one of the earliest speculative bubbles to form, and it had also been one of the first to start losing air.

Amazingly, Merrill Lynch decided this was the perfect time to double its bet on subprime lending and perhaps to dump Ownit. On September 5, 2006, Dallas got the shock of his life when Merrill announced that it would buy First Franklin for $1.3 billion. Even as Michael Blum had been sitting on Ownit's board, he and other Merrill executives had been on the hunt for a bigger subprime lender to buy.

In a press release announcing the deal, Blum was quoted as saying that First Franklin "fills an important gap for us" by providing "a significant presence in both the wholesale and online retail channels." That seemed to be a direct slap at Dallas, who wondered what kind of "gap" Ownit was supposed to fill.

Dallas was furious. "They never consulted with me," he said. Though he had started First Franklin and had been its chief executive as recently as 2001, he considered it a direct competitor. Over the next three months, Dallas found himself wrangling more and more with Merrill Lynch. Far from coming to the rescue as his senior partners, Blum and Whalen were demanding that Ownit buy back another $165 million in problem mortgages.

Dallas started angling to let Merrill Lynch take over Ownit entirely, without paying an extra dime, if it would absorb the liabilities and keep it going. By this time the Merrill executives were fixated completely on First Franklin, a much bigger mortgage lender that didn't seem to have Ownit's problems. "We had survived the tsunami at Aceh," Dallas said, referring to the earthquake-induced tidal wave that killed thousands of people at the Indonesian resort of Aceh. "But we didn't see the real problem, which was First Franklin."

At the start of December 2006, Merrill Lynch and JPMorgan Chase, which was Ownit's other big warehouse lender, both refused to fund Ownit's mortgages. Dallas frantically called both companies. JPMorgan Chase executives told him he needed to "stand behind" his mortgages, which meant taking all the risk if they were kicked back by investors. Dallas couldn't do that, but he had thought the deal to let Merrill take over Ownit was almost done. That would have resolved all the fights at one time. Despite assurances from Merrill, Dallas said, one day after another passed without any resolution.

By December 7, Dallas had had enough. In a move that shocked his employees and probably his erstwhile partners at Merrill—but delighted executives at First Franklin—Ownit filed for bankruptcy and closed its doors.

Merrill Lynch executives refused to talk about Dallas or Ownit. Matthew Whalen quietly quit Merrill in May 2007, and Michael Blum was pushed out in May 2008. "The important thing is that all the people who were involved in that strategy are now gone," Jessica Oppenheim, a spokeswoman for Merrill Lynch, told me a few months after Blum had left.

By that time, Merrill Lynch had become the poster child for self-destructive excesses. First Franklin began to founder almost as soon as Merrill Lynch completed the acquisition in January 2007. Though First Franklin appeared to have much lower default rates than Ownit had, that was largely because National City Bank had kept many of the most troubled mortgages on its own books before selling the subprime lender to Merrill.

After the acquisition, Merrill hardly reined in the risk taking. Wayne Bereman, an underwriter at First Franklin in Cleveland both before and after the takeover, said the change was dramatic. Though First Franklin had been relaxing its lending standards regularly for two years, Merrill Lynch not only picked up the pace but drastically raised the loan production quotas for account executives. "Normally, you don't get new underwriting instructions more than once a month," Bereman said. "But we were getting some kind of new instruction almost every day, usually to make things looser."

Bereman found himself under relentless pressure to make exceptions and approve as many loans as possible. "If I rejected an application, the account executive would immediately come and complain to my boss about how unreasonable I was," Bereman recounted. If that didn't work, the sales rep would go to his own boss, who would appeal to higher management for an "exception" to the rules. "They would make you feel miserable," Bereman said. "And even if I absolutely dug in and said no, there were some applications that got approved anyway."

Between easier standards and higher production quotas, it was only a matter of months before First Franklin's default rates and "kick-outs" started climbing as well. By that time, investors had already become frightened by an early wave of subprime collapses, especially the huge bankruptcy of New Century Financial in April 2007.

In August, when the subprime crisis metastasized into a broader financial meltdown, all of Stanley O'Neal and Merrill's horrendous bets on the housing market were going bad at the same time: its mortgages, its investment in First Franklin, and most of all its $30 billion inventory of collateralized debt obligations.

At First Franklin, life went from bad to miserable for thousands of employees, many of whom had worked at the company for years. When Stanley O'Neal was fired as chairman and chief executive of Merrill Lynch in October 2007, few felt any satisfaction that he had lost his job before they lost theirs. In November, Merrill laid off account executives without any warning and without any severance pay. At the Mortgage Lender Implode-O-Meter, a website that became one of the definitive chroniclers of collapsing subprime lenders, enraged First Franklin employees blasted "mother Merrill" and O'Neal in thousands of postings.

Amid all the fury, however, one First Franklin blogger saw the opportunity for grim humor. "No one likes to see people out of a job," he wrote. "But Bill Dallas has to be somewhere, laughing his ass off."

11

PUBLIC FLAILING,
PRIVATE FAILING

My two worlds—the professional one, in which I reported on the nation's mortgage crisis; and my personal one, where I was neck-deep in a mortgage crisis and a marriage crisis—started to collide in August 2007.

When the growing panic over subprime loans ruptured the wider credit markets, the mortgage crisis shot to the top of Washington's political agenda and to the top of my reporting assignments. It was sad that it took a crisis on Wall Street to focus the White House and the Federal Reserve on the woes of the housing sector. Even Democratic leaders in Congress, who were perhaps more reflexively inclined to rescue troubled home owners, had focused on other things.

The onset of a broader economic crisis snapped all of Washington to attention and exposed the flawed ideas and complacency that had been building for years. The "resilience" and "flexibility" of

the US economy, traits long trumpeted by both the Bush administration and Fed officials, had found their limits. Having rebounded
from one shock after another—the Asian financial crisis of the late
1990s, the dot-com collapse in 2000, the terrorist attacks of 2001,
the recession and slow recovery—investors and policy makers alike
seemed to think that setbacks were just hiccups on the way to even
higher growth.

The core belief in the economy's ability to bounce back was cou-
pled with the equally dangerous idea that a free-market economy
was self-correcting, and that rational self-interest would rein in
self-destructive excess and fraud. Less regulation was always better than more. In fact, banking regulators, like the Office of Thrift
Supervision and the Office of the Comptroller of the Currency,
referred to financial institutions as "clients" and competed against
each other for market share.

A bigger intellectual weakness was becoming apparent—one
more widespread than faith in flexibility and free markets: mainstream economists didn't know what to do about irrational behavior,
which put them at a huge disadvantage in dealing with speculative
bubbles. Nobody denied that bubbles had been a fact of life, or
that they were by definition irrational. In a bubble, people bid up
the price of an asset—tulips, gold, tech stocks, real estate—not
because they believe its underlying value has increased but because
they believe other speculators will bid the price up even higher.
Bubbles share some of the characteristics of a Ponzi scheme, in
that the players reap profits only as long as new players keep bringing in more money. Once the number of new players hits a plateau,
the bubble pops and the bust follows.

Because bubbles embody the opposite of rational self-interest,
many mainstream economists had an almost irrational bias against
dealing with them. Both Greenspan and Bernanke had made logi-

cal and pragmatic cases for how difficult it was to distinguish a bubble from a price increase on the basis of "fundamental" changes. They argued for cleanup rather than prevention. But the truth was that grappling with an irrational mania violated two core articles of faith for mainstream economists: don't second-guess investors, and don't intervene in the markets.

Under normal circumstances, I would have loved nothing more than to ride this bull of a story. A banking system that had all but shut down. Wall Street in ruins. Greed, sleaze, and a president who kept insisting that the "fundamentals of the economy are sound." For an economics reporter it doesn't get any better than that. Yet it was hard to be exhilarated by a national meltdown when I was in the middle of a personal one. Patty and I were hurtling toward default on our mortgage, the foreclosure on our house, and quite possibly the end of our marriage. The financial strain was poisoning us, each in our own way. Patty's inability or unwillingness to earn more money enraged me, and she felt trapped and terrified by a man who seemed like Captain Queeg, if not Jabba the Hutt.

We hadn't yet gone more than thirty days delinquent on the mortgage, but we were behind on everything else. Bill collectors were calling six days a week, starting promptly at 8:00 a.m. "Telemarketers," I would mumble when my son Matthew asked why we got so many robocalls from 800 numbers. Our stately little house looked increasingly trashy: peeling paint and broken screens on the front windows; crumbling concrete on the front stoop; a lawn that was mostly crabgrass. The furniture that Patty had salvaged from her first marriage was falling apart. The cotton slipcovers on the sofa and armchair were in shreds. The frosted-crystal shade on a beloved Italian floor lamp was cracked. The dog had gnawed the leg on her Biedermeier chair.

We were staying afloat, sort of, with help from a stream of occasional and hard-to-predict windfalls: a fat tax refund over here, thanks to our humongous mortgage interest deductions; a $5,000 bonus over there, thanks to the *Times*; twice-yearly payouts for the extra days I worked. And despite President Bush's attempts to slash wasteful federal spending on child support enforcement, California's child support agency had intercepted $2,700 in tax refunds from Patty's ex-husband. Ka-ching!

In late July 2007, just as the credit markets were first seizing up, a taxi sideswiped our car and we received a check for $2,200 from the driver's insurance company. Instead of getting the car fixed, we left the dents where they were and used the money to pay bills. None of that changed our basic trajectory. We were sinking, and we were probably sinking faster than before.

It was strange and sometimes awkward to report about a nation-wide disaster while in the midst of my own. I didn't care that my one remaining suit was wearing out, or that each of my blazers was missing at least one button. I had been a subprime dresser long before I became a subprime borrower. On the beat, however, I was becoming angrier, more exhausted, and a lot less eager to be evenhanded.

I liked Ben S. Bernanke, Greenspan's successor at the Federal Reserve, and I appreciated the refreshing pragmatism of Treasury Secretary Henry M. Paulson Jr. What I couldn't believe was the arrogant, dogmatic, and incompetent economic team in the Bush White House. When Republicans and President Bush blamed the mortgage crisis on irresponsible borrowers, I wanted to scream out, "Sure, blame us! You were the guys who wanted Wall Street and the commercial banks to run wild, until you started denouncing their 'greed.' You were the ones who kept bragging about the record home ownership. And you were the guys who nearly doubled the national debt to $10 trillion in eight short years."

This was the first time I had reported on issues in which I had a personal stake. I wondered if this was what it felt like to be a pregnant woman who had to report on the political battle over abortion. Half of the people I interviewed thought borrowers like me were the scum of the earth. On the other hand, a lot of the people in my own situation seemed a little scummy themselves. No one seemed objective.

I was getting uncomfortably close to a conflict of interest, particularly as Congress and the Bush administration began battling over how to help troubled home owners.

John Taylor, a veteran advocate of low-income housing who had grown up in Boston's projects, had been one of the earliest champions of a sweeping bailout for subprime borrowers.

Over lunch at a Chinese restaurant near my office in December 2007, Taylor argued that the federal government could solve a big part of the crisis if it put up $100 billion and refinanced subprime borrowers into cheaper government-guaranteed loans. If you persuaded a lender to reduce the outstanding balance on a loan in exchange for being able to sell it and get it off its books, the government would eventually get most of its money back, Taylor claimed.

"$100 billion!" I said. "You can't be serious."

"It will cost the government a lot more than that if the country goes into a serious recession," he retorted. "And if we don't get the housing market turned around, that's what we're going to have."

The issue put me in a tricky position as a reporter. If I stood a chance of being bailed out by Washington, my financial straits could pose a conflict of interest that would taint my reporting. It was hard to imagine any politician voting to bail out a white, well-educated newspaper reporter who earned $130,000 a year and had borrowed twice as much as he could afford. Bush certainly wouldn't. I probably wouldn't myself.

Yet these were crazy times. Anything was possible.

Like other big newspapers, *The New York Times* has stringent prohibitions against conflicts of interest. Its reporters cannot own stock in the companies we write about. We cannot take gifts or earn money from people or institutions we write about. We aren't supposed to have a personal stake in the outcome of events we write about. (There are exceptions: reporters covering horse races are free to place wagers.) As far as I knew, though, no one had ever asked whether a reporter's financial position might influence his coverage on a policy debate. Our ethics manual was silent on the matter.

The issue eventually came up just after Thanksgiving 2007, when I drafted a proposal for this book and sent a copy to our standards editor, Craig Whitney. Under our rules, staff members had to show any book proposals to the *Times* and give the paper a chance to bid on the book as well. The *Times* passed on the book, but Whitney wondered about my situation. "Can you really keep covering this issue if you're personally involved?" he wrote me. "I meant to say earlier that I'm really sorry you're in this mess, which to me shows the crying need for regulation of this kind of gross malpractice, if not fraud. But since you are, don't you have a conflict of interest if you're reporting on it?"

My gut feeling was that the political and policy debates wouldn't have any impact on me, one way or another. On the off chance I was affected, I would face the same kind of issue as a reporter covering the debate over a middle-class tax cut. Since almost all reporters stood to gain from that kind of tax cut, nobody would be left to report on the debate if they all recused themselves. Whitney agreed, though he added that I should recuse myself from any stories involving my own mortgage lenders.

To say that Washington was unprepared for the crisis was a huge understatement.

On August 8, 2007, as stock and bond markets were gyrating wildly over worries about the mortgage meltdown, President Bush appeared at the Treasury Department. As he delivered his prepared remarks in front of TV cameras, he failed to mention the panic in credit markets that was at the top of investors' minds. Instead, he reprised his standard economic stump speech: the importance of his tax cuts; the virtues of entrepreneurship; the need for Congress to pass the free-trade agreements his administration had negotiated. He then boasted about the millions of new jobs created since 2003 and about the economy's strength. "Not only is our economy strong, but so is [sic] the economies around the world," Bush said, displaying his penchant for fractured grammar.

When reporters asked Bush about the turmoil on Wall Street over rising foreclosures, the president breezily answered that the tumult was part of a "necessary correction" to the "flood of liquidity" that had entered the United States. Struggling home owners were one of the causes of the meltdown, he added, because many hadn't read the "fine print" on their mortgages. "There needs [sic] to be financial education measures in place," he said.

Below the surface, Fed and Treasury officials were scrambling to come up with ways to deal with what suddenly looked like an epic calamity. Three weeks after Bush's peculiar appearance at the Treasury, he stood in the Rose Garden to announce a plan called "FHA Secure" to help subprime borrowers. As analysts had been warning for months, well over two million families were at risk of losing their homes because their monthly payments on subprime loans were about to explode.

Officials claimed that FHA Secure, a new wrinkle to the Federal Housing Administration's mortgage insurance program, would help refinance 240,000 subprime borrowers and as many as 60,000 people who were already delinquent. Even as advertised, the program would have been a token gesture directed toward fewer than 10 percent of those at risk of losing their homes. According to an analysis by Rachel Swarns at *The New York Times*, only 150,000 people had received any help by the following April, some 90,000 fewer than had been advertised. The plan to stabilize 60,000 families who were already delinquent on their loans also fell short. The program had made loans to only 1,792 such people.

It was hard to overstate how inept Bush and some of his top advisers were in reacting to the housing crisis. Alphonso Jackson, the secretary for Housing and Urban Development (HUD), complained at a Senate hearing in October 2007 that many people facing foreclosure were "yuppies" who didn't deserve help. Jackson had made headlines during Bush's first term by publicly declaring that he didn't see any need to award contracts to people who didn't support Bush. Then he came under federal investigation over allegations that HUD had doled out lucrative contracts to his friends and business associates. Jackson asserted that he had done nothing wrong, but he refused to answer questions in public about the issues. He resigned in April 2008. The federal investigation still appeared to be under way at the end of 2008, but officials offered no clues about whether it would lead to charges or fizzle out.

For practical purposes, Bush had already handed responsibility for the entire crisis over to Henry Paulson and the Treasury Department. Paulson brought enormous stamina and a refreshing pragmatism to his job, but he was flailing too. A former chairman of Goldman Sachs who had been a linebacker for Dartmouth College's football team, Paulson prided himself on charging headfirst into any crisis that came his way. He talked quickly, often changing directions in midsentence, and seemed to thrive on urgency and quick action. Paulson was less of a thinker than a deal cutter, either despite or because of his years as head of one of Wall Street's most respected investment banks. His preferred approach to solving a problem was to corral the key players in a single room, force them to brainstorm together, and then bang enough heads to produce what others would call a "win-win" solution.

Like Bush, Paulson insisted that the "fundamentals of the economy are sound" well past the end of 2007. Where others saw a broad economic calamity involving millions of overstretched home owners and staggering losses throughout the financial system, Paulson saw practical bottlenecks in the financial system. Partly as a result, he opposed forcing financial companies to do things they didn't want to do. He also opposed spending large amounts of tax-payer money to aggressively modify mortgages, which smacked of a bailout for people who had made bad decisions.

Paulson instead focused much of his early energy on Hope Now, a voluntary group of the biggest mortgage-servicing companies and securitizers that was supposed to speed up efforts to modify subprime loans. Its director was Faith Schwartz, a former lobbyist for Option One, a subprime lender owned by H&R Block. The goal of Hope Now was to reach out to troubled borrowers and get them to talk to their lenders. Those who did make the call discovered that the lenders weren't making any specific commitments, and the lenders made it clear they were interested in making concessions only if it would cost them less money than a foreclosure.

To Paulson, this seemed like a perfect win-win way to prevent foreclosures. Industry analysts estimated that between sinking home prices and the time and money it took to foreclose on a house, lenders were likely to lose about half of the original loan amount on every subprime foreclosure. "Foreclosure isn't only expensive for home owners," Paulson told listeners in December 2007, at a town meeting in Stockton, California, a city with one of the highest foreclosure rates in the United States. "Investors would rather find a solution other than foreclosure, if there is one." On top of that, he added proudly, his solution "involves no government funding or subsidies for industry or home owners."

Despite the hoopla, Hope Now had virtually no impact. At the end of 2008, more than a full year after it was under way, the Mortgage Bankers Association of America estimated that a record 2.2 million homes had entered foreclosure proceedings that year. That number was up by half from 1.5 million foreclosure starts in 2007 and more than double the 960,000 recorded in 2006. In fact, foreclosure rates had climbed to new records in every category of home loan, including traditional mortgages to prime borrowers. Among subprime borrowers, the group that Hope Now was supposed to help, one out of eight homes was in foreclosure.

———

The panic attack hit me around 2:00 a.m. on Patty's birthday. It was October 17, 2007, and I was lying in bed obsessing over bills that couldn't be postponed and the money we didn't have to pay them. Like many of my predawn fear cascades, this one had its start with a specific unpaid bill: $240 in traffic tickets—$140 for speeding, $50 each for expired tags and inspection. The fines would double if we didn't pay them in less than a week. The tickets had uncorked the bottle on all the other "must pays": the $400 electric bill with the cutoff date printed in red; the $220 cable/telephone/ Internet bill for the past two months; the MasterCard and American Express bills—at least one of which had to be brought current or I wouldn't even be able to travel for work. And of course, there was the $3,271 mortgage payment.

My panic circuitry was in fine form, connecting small debts to big ones, short-term problems to the bottomless abyss, private calamity to public shame. Most of the time, I could ignore the fears amid the familiar pressures of newspaper reporting, the demands of children, and the delights of sex. Once Patty was asleep and I was alone in the dark, though, the bottled-up fear reached the surface and gave me insomnia for the first time in my life. I tossed from side to side, trying to figure out at least a triage plan for our bills. I was too fidgety to lie still in bed, but I was in no mood to actually sit down with the bills themselves. I climbed out of bed for a moment, then jumped back in. I couldn't decide if I would rather feel confined or all alone.

Patty woke up, irritated by all my movement and my occasional moans of despair. "What's the matter?" she asked.

"I can't sleep," I answered. "I'm panicking about money, because I don't know how we're going to pay all the bills that need to be paid right now." I wanted her to take me in her arms and somehow reassure me that everything would be OK. But that wasn't happening.

"There's nothing you can do about it right now," she answered sleepily.

"If this keeps on, we're going to lose the house," I persisted, sounding less panicked and more petulant. If Patty wouldn't give me comfort, then I wanted her to suffer alongside me. "I don't know how we're going to make it. We can't go on like this."

Patty had begged me to grant her a birthday reprieve from my nagging and kvetching over money issues. What I saw as an uncontrollable moment of panic, she saw as another deliberate attempt to browbeat her.

"I can't believe you are doing this to me on my birthday," she hissed in fury. "All I had asked for was one day of peace—*one day* when you weren't beating me over the head. And here it is, not even daylight yet, and you're waking me up to berate me about money."

"Son of a bitch, what did I do to you?" I asked, punching my pillow in the dark. "Do you think I enjoy having a panic attack? I can't help what I'm feeling. I'm just scared out of my mind."

"That's it!" Patty snapped, getting out of bed and pulling on her robe. "I'm not going to listen to any more of this. I'm going to sleep downstairs."

It sounded like a two-minute dust-up, but it wasn't.

"You lied to me," she told me as I got coffee in the morning. "You said that what I saw on the outside was pretty much what you were. But you're completely different. If I had known what you were really like, I would never have come out here."

I've married a lunatic, I thought. She's gone nutters. It's as if I had drugged her in LA, thrown her into the trunk of my car, and forced her to start making money as a hooker in Washington. What was next? The head-turning scene from *The Exorcist*?

I wasn't Captain Queeg. I was a schmuck who was broke and needed her help. I had spent months trying to avoid provoking her about how much money she made. I had run up insane amounts of debt to keep the dream alive, and I was tapped out. I had even written her a long letter in which I tried to imagine her anger toward me entirely through her eyes.

I had been a first-class prick on plenty of occasions—that was true. During one of our early fights over money shortly after buying the house, I had threatened to take away the credit cards I had given her. I had berated and blamed her for our financial problems, and had accused her of hiding from reality. I had thrown pillows, pens, and eyeglasses (my own, as it happened) across the bedroom. I had punched a crack in the solid-wood door of her antique wardrobe—while she was standing in front of it.

Patty was exhausted, frightened, and in despair. She was certain that I regretted the day she had come to Washington, and that I was much angrier at her than I ever admitted. She was terrified that I would erupt without warning into a rage worse than anything she had seen before.

Meanwhile, she was working and sleeping in a house that was noisy, cramped, often dirty, and in growing disrepair. The summer had been particularly brutal, with teenagers traipsing through the house and leaving debris in their wake. Almost every room needed a fresh coat of paint. The basement carpet was moldy and the outside gutters were jammed up, causing water to spill down the side of the house. We didn't have money to fix any of it.

It was a long way down from her elegant and spacious former home in Los Angeles. Patty didn't complain about my modest salary as a *Times* reporter. She did miss the housekeeper who had come several times a week and her once-dazzling wardrobe. She deeply missed her older boys, who had stayed on the West Coast.

What she missed most of all, she remarked during calmer moments, was the joy she had gotten from me when I first courted her. Back then, I seemed passionate, courageous, intelligent, and wildly in love with her. Now I was snappy, distant, prone to rage, and often barely aware of her. "Time will erode our miraculous love if you cannot allow me to be myself and love all of me, even if I don't become the brilliant, glamorous career woman you imagined," she had warned me in an email a few months before my panic. "We are both old enough to know that even true love doesn't guarantee bliss."

Now she was so wounded that her fight-or-flight reflex had taken over. She wanted to get as far away from me as she could but she had no money, no place to go, and a beloved little girl who didn't deserve any more trauma. She was convinced she was trapped with a madman.

"It's so noble-sounding for you to tell everyone that you love me," she wrote me two days after my panic. "But the facts are that you chose to behave in a way that has made it impossible for our so-called marriage to survive. You have been unforgivably cruel, which I'm sure is left out of the story. . . . I have learned the hard way that your indifference to ending your first marriage was a manifestation of your coldness and abusiveness. I keep asking myself how I missed it, or failed to focus on the things that might have saved me."

Five days after my panic, Patty and I sat at a kitchen table with Susan and Peter Kilborn, in the same house in which we had been married. Susan had persuaded us to sit down with her on the pretext of reviewing options on our house. Susan's great gift was her quiet patience and her ability to let people be themselves. She had a way of saying very little but letting you know that she cared. She had insisted that she would not play the mediator in our marital battle. She would just give us a chance to talk through the practical issues.

"I put together a little research," Susan said, displaying printouts of recent home sales and rental prices in our area. We had three options, she told us. We could rent the house out to other people and move into a less expensive house or apartment. Or we could try to sell the house entirely. Or we could try to stay in the house by bringing in extra money. There was a fourth option—turning the keys over to JPMorgan Chase and letting the mortgage foreclose. Susan, showing a Machiavellian shrewdness in framing the discussion, didn't mention that one.

Not surprisingly, the prospects for selling the house or renting it out did not look good. Sale prices hadn't dropped much in the area, but most houses were sitting on the market for months without getting offers. "You'll have to put money into the house to get it ready," Susan noted. Since money was exactly what we didn't have, we would be at an immediate disadvantage in bargaining for top dollar.

Then there was the matter of our $472,000 mortgage. That had been equal to 95 percent of the home's appraised value in mid-2006, at the peak of the housing bubble. And while the appraisal of $500,000 hadn't been off-the-charts crazy, the appraiser had been hired by our mortgage broker and knew what number we needed to hit. It would take real luck to get $500,000 now. Even if we did, we would still have to give up 6 percent in commissions to the real estate agents. Bottom line: we probably wouldn't escape without losing thousands of dollars we did not have.

The rental option wasn't much better. Rental prices on similar houses in the area were between $2,200 and $2,500 per month. If we could get that higher number, we would still need to come up with almost $800 a month, on top of whatever rent we were paying on a house or apartment.

"That brings us to trying to stay in the house," Susan said, looking at both Patty and me.

The one piece of good news was that my alimony payments were scheduled to end in February, so my monthly take-home pay would jump by $1,000, increasing to $3,300 a month—almost exactly the same amount as our mortgage payment. "What is the minimum you need to meet your basic expenses?" Susan asked.

I thought we needed at least $3,000, but we might be able to skate by on $2,500 for a short while if we didn't use any money for entertainment or even Christmas gifts, and if we were lucky enough to escape any unexpected repair bills for the car or house.

"Patty, do you think you can bring in $2,500 a month?" Susan asked. Patty had been listening in silence through most of this. Slowly, hesitantly, she nodded.

12

REVERSE REDLINING

When Miguel and Ana Delgado (not their real names) bought their supersized, five-bedroom dream house near Manassas, Virginia, it was as if they had parachuted into an episode of *Cribs*. With five thousand square feet of interior space, the brick-veneer colonial came with all the luxuries of late-bubble, tract-mansion architecture. It had a two-car garage, a two-story foyer, and a two-person Jacuzzi in a master bathroom that was bigger than my living room. The kitchen, with solid-cherry cabinets and top-of-the-line appliances, opened out to the "great room" with its cathedral ceiling. The house even had a theater room worthy of Tony Soprano.

The Delgados, who had emigrated from El Salvador with virtually no money in 1986, bought their new home for $720,000 in 2005. They had put down $72,000 of their own money, the profit from selling their first house, and borrowed the rest with a "1 percent" mortgage from Countrywide Financial. They dutifully wrote a $2,800 check each month to pay for it.

By the time I met them in June 2008, their dream house had become a nightmare. Their mortgage was $80,000 higher than when they had started and the value of their house was $185,000 lower. The actual monthly payment on their mortgage, they had belatedly discovered, had never been $2,800. It had been $6,000. The option ARM they had signed allowed for a "minimum payment" of only $2,800. Every time they mailed a check for that amount, they had been borrowing another $3,200 and adding that to their total loan.

"We didn't think we were doing anything risky," Miguel said. "We thought we could manage it."

It took them a year to realize their mistake, and when they did they were already trapped. They couldn't afford to stay, but they couldn't sell the house for anything close to what they had paid. "We've lost everything—the house, our down payment, all our savings," said Miguel, a painting and drywall contractor.

He and Ana were sitting in the office of Maribel Alvarez, a real estate agent in Manassas who was negotiating a "short-sale" agreement with Countrywide. Miguel still struggled with English, even though he and Ana had become US citizens years earlier. For almost two years, they had searched for some way to keep their home. They had even refinanced their original mortgage, only to end up with another option ARM from Countrywide. Now they were giving up.

Alvarez, who ran a storefront brokerage called Info Senter Realty, had found a buyer willing to pay $535,000 for their house. Under the short-sale agreement she had drawn up, Countrywide would finance the new buyer and drop its claim to the remaining $205,000 that the Delgados owed. Ana and Miguel would turn over the keys in July and move with their children into a two-bedroom rental house.

"How could you have thought that you could buy a house for $720,000 and only pay $2,800 a month?" I asked.

"If someone speaks the same language as you, you feel you can trust them," Miguel answered. Their real estate agent had been so confident, assuring them they could easily trade up from their starter house to a palace. It had been easy too. She had sold their first house for a good price, and her husband, a mortgage broker, had quickly lined up their loan. And since they had all come from Central America, the Delgados didn't delve into the details.

The Delgados were hardly alone. Hispanic families, drawn by the comparatively affordable prices for homes in quiet suburbs, had flocked by the thousands to Manassas and other parts of Prince William County. By 2008, they were losing their homes in stunning numbers. Foreclosures and forced home sales were off the charts, and neighborhoods were emptying out. The average sale price for single-family homes in several Manassas zip codes crashed by 33 percent between the middle of 2007 and the middle of 2008.

Neighborhoods that had been stable for decades suddenly looked as if they had been hit by neutron bombs: the houses were still standing, but the people were gone. In West Gate of Lomond, a subdivision of brick ramblers built in the 1960s, almost every block had at least one house in foreclosure and two or three more on the brink.

In Baldwin Oaks, a '70s-era subdivision, the lawns were all trimmed and the local tennis courts were in good shape. But when I pulled into a cul-de-sac with ten homes on it, the illusion evaporated. One house had an unmistakable scarlet letter: a sign announcing the house's auction date. Four others had lockboxes on their front doors and were uninhabited. Another two had "For

Sale" and "Price Reduced" signs. Though precise numbers were hard to come by, it was clear that Hispanic families were being hit hard.

Manassas was best known as the site of the First Battle of Bull Run, the first major battle of the Civil War. In its new guise as a magnet for Hispanic migrants, it was a case study in how the mortgage industry had turned old-fashioned racial profiling on its head. For decades, civil rights groups and community groups had accused banks and finance companies of "redlining," drawing real or metaphorical lines around predominantly black neighborhoods and refusing to lend there. Over the years, redlining had become a broad metaphor for discrimination against borrowers based on their race or ethnic background.

The explosive growth of subprime lending had rendered old-fashioned redlining moot. In the new era, lenders weren't rejecting customers whom they considered high-risk. They were aggressively seeking them, because risky customers were the only ones willing to pay higher rates and fees. If blacks or recent immigrants were dodgier borrowers, that was actually a point in their favor.

Subprime and Alt-A mortgage lenders made a huge push into Manassas and Prince William County and targeted Hispanic customers. The lenders advertised heavily in Spanish-language newspapers and on Spanish-language radio stations and cable networks. They recruited Latino mortgage brokers and real estate agents, dangling sales commissions—known as "yield-spread premiums," or YSPs—that were at least two times as generous for subprime loans as the ones for traditional mortgages. On my own dodgy Fremont mortgage, Bob Andrews' company Vertex Financial had been paid a handsome YSP.

"The lenders would have their reps come into your office every week, telling you they had the answer to your clients' problems," said Jose Semidey, who owned a real estate brokerage called Pan American Real Estate in Tysons Corner, Virginia. "They kept talking about how much money you could make on the YSP." The typical yield-spread premium was at least 2.5 percent of the mortgage amount, and it often went higher. On a modest $200,000 mortgage, that could mean $5,000 for less than a day's work. By contrast, the commission on a conventional mortgage was usually 1 percent or less.

In 2005 and 2006, as the housing frenzy was reaching its fevered peak, 31 percent of all mortgages in the city of Manassas were subprime loans, according to data collected by the Center for Responsible Lending. That was a far higher concentration than for Virginia's statewide average of 22.4 percent, and that number didn't even include the burgeoning number of option ARMs and other junk loans to prime borrowers like Miguel and Ana.

Jose Semidey worked closely with his brother, Rafael, who had become a "superbroker," a mortgage broker so prolific that lenders gave him his own credit line so that he could close on mortgages himself. "We did a lot of no-income-verification loans and 2/28's," Jose Semidey admitted with regret. "But when you do a no-income-verification loan, you're setting a person up for failure. With predatory lending, we brewed the perfect storm."

Lenders also targeted black home buyers. Cities and counties with large concentrations of African-American residents routinely had extraordinarily high percentages of subprime mortgages. In Prince George's County, Maryland, which had become a magnet for upwardly mobile blacks who wanted to move out of Washington DC, 41 percent of all mortgages were subprime in 2005 and 2006. In Baltimore, 46 percent of all mortgages were subprime.

From big cities like Chicago and Cleveland to Stockton, California, the patterns were strikingly similar. African-Americans and Hispanics were several times more likely than whites to get subprime mortgages, even when the borrowers had comparable incomes. Not surprisingly, foreclosure rates from subprime loans were heavily concentrated in communities with high percentages of blacks and immigrants.

Mortgage and real estate executives argued that the disparities simply reflected lower incomes and financial straits that had nothing to do with racial or ethnic targeting by lenders. Far from exploiting disadvantaged groups, supporters of subprime lending said it had opened doors for them and dramatically boosted home ownership among blacks, Latinos, and other ethnic minorities.

It was true that subprime lending had caused at least a temporary surge in home ownership among minorities. From 1994 to 2004, the home ownership rate among black Americans jumped from 42 to 49 percent—an increase of more than 1 million households, according to data from the US Census Bureau. The home ownership rate among Hispanics jumped from 41 to almost 47 percent, an increase of almost 2 million households.

That was great, except that many of those benefits turned out to be illusory.

Despite my own mortgage predicament—or possibly because of my own predicament, which I considered self-inflicted—my personal bias was to heap at least equal blame on borrowers as on lenders and Wall Street securitizers when the whole business finally blew up. Just because somebody offered to sell you the rope to hang yourself didn't mean you had to buy it. Adults were supposed to take responsibility for their decisions, and although subprime mortgages and option ARMs were complicated, a person didn't need a PhD in mathematics to understand their basic risks.

It wasn't a secret that the teaser rates would expire. That's why they're called teaser rates. If your take-home pay was $3,000 a month and you knew your subprime mortgage had a solid chance of jumping from $1,500 a month to $2,000, why should anyone rescue you if that actually came to pass?

As it happened, subprime borrowers seemed to have a surprisingly good idea about how the system worked. A study by Eric Rosengren, president of the Federal Reserve Bank of Boston, noted that 71 percent of all subprime borrowers in 2004 paid off their loans within two years. The borrowers might have sold their homes, refinanced with a cheaper loan, or simply refinanced with another subprime loan. One way or another, though, most borrowers understood the teaser rates well enough to bail out of their loans before their rates jumped.

But there was more to it than that.

Edward Gramlich, the late Federal Reserve governor who had analyzed the benefits and dangers of subprime lending for years, remarked that mortgage lenders had aimed their most baffling products at the customers who were least likely to understand them. "Why are the most risky loan products sold to the least sophisticated borrowers?" Gramlich wrote in a speech he prepared just before he died in September 2007. "The question answers itself—the least sophisticated borrowers are probably duped into taking these products."

On the surface, it seemed hard to sympathize with people who became trapped by option ARMs. If you were paying only $2,800 a month on a mortgage of $650,000, something was up. Miguel and Ana squirmed, but they didn't concede the point. Who were they to judge what was strange? After all, the soaring value of their first house had put $72,000 in their hands. If that was possible, it might not be impossible to have a $2,800 monthly payment on a beautiful home. This was America. Anything could happen.

Nor were the Delgados alone in their confusion. Maribel Alvarez, the real estate agent who was trying to extricate them and other
clients from such loans, confessed that she herself had arranged
option ARMs for a few clients before she fully understood all the
implications. "I have to admit that I did a few of those loans," she
said. "I didn't really understand how they worked."

Whoever was to blame, there wasn't anything new about the
"new" redlining. As early as 2000, long before subprime mortgages truly exploded on the scene, the Department of Housing
and Urban Development (HUD) bluntly warned that unscrupulous lenders were steering black borrowers into high-cost mortgages, even though many qualified for cheaper and safer loans. In
a detailed analysis of lending patterns in eight major cities, HUD
found the same pattern time and time again: regardless of their
income levels, black borrowers were far more likely than whites
to end up with subprime loans. In Los Angeles, HUD reported,
upper-income black borrowers who refinanced their homes were
almost twice as likely as *low-income* whites to end up with subprime
loans. In Chicago, home owners in middle-income, predominantly
black neighborhoods were six times as likely to have subprime loans
as home owners in middle-income white neighborhoods.

The HUD reports were remarkably prescient, warning that
deceptive and possibly abusive loan practices had arisen alongside
legitimate subprime lending and that many of the lenders oper-
ated almost entirely outside the reach of federal banking regulators. "There is a growing body of anecdotal evidence," HUD wrote
in 2000, "that a subset of these subprime lenders, who generally
operate outside the federal regulatory structure, engage in abusive
lending practices that strip borrowers' home equity and place them
at increased risk of foreclosure."

Ellen Seidman, then director of the Office of Thrift Supervision, argued that one reason such a disproportionate share of subprime loans went to African-Americans was simply that subprime lenders were often the only game in town for them. "Many of those served by the subprime market are creditworthy borrowers who are simply stuck with subprime loans or subprime lenders because they live in neighborhoods that have too few credit or banking opportunities," Seidman told a conference of community bankers in April 2000.

For a well-positioned subprime mortgage broker with ties to the local community, there was almost no competition. If brokers had a chance to choose between making a 1 percent commission on a prime loan or a 2.5 percent commission on a subprime loan, it isn't hard to guess how often they took less money.

All of these warnings came before go-go lending began its golden era of mind-boggling growth around 2002 and before lenders abandoned every last shred of caution in 2005 and 2006.

The patterns of discrimination didn't get much better when "respectable" banks like Citigroup and Washington Mutual and "respectable" Wall Street firms like Merrill Lynch jumped into the fray. Though the Federal Reserve staunchly refused to do anything about abuses in subprime lending, its own data gave ammunition to critics who charged that subprime lending exploited African-Americans and immigrants.

Drawing on data provided by more than eighty-eight hundred lenders under the Home Mortgage Disclosure Act, the Fed reported in 2005 that regardless of income level, black borrowers were almost three times as likely as whites to have subprime mortgages.

About 39 percent of all low-income black borrowers had subprime loans, compared to only 12 percent of low-income whites.

Among high-income borrowers, whom the Fed defined as individuals earning more than 120 percent of the median income in their region, 29 percent of black borrowers had high-cost mortgages, compared to 17 percent of Hispanics and only 5.8 percent of whites. Industry executives argued that the statistics didn't prove anything, especially since the Fed hadn't collected any data about borrowers' credit scores.

"To us, it seemed they were saying you could explain the majority of the differences," Douglas Duncan, then the chief economist at the Mortgage Bankers Association, told me at the time. "You would expect to see, higher-priced loans in higher-priced categories."

The statistics were dry, even mind-numbing, and they couldn't clinch the case. To do that would require on-the-street investigations, and nobody—not the Bush administration, not the Federal Reserve, and not even Democratic leaders in Congress—showed any interest.

Yet there was so much data, year after year, and it always pointed in the same direction. It reinforced the anecdotal experiences of families like the Delgados: people on the outskirts of the financial system who were timid were being steered by people they trusted, who in turn had been recruited by the big lenders precisely because of their ethnic ties.

"The worst part of this is that Hispanic home owners were being victimized by Hispanic brokers," said Miguel Avila, a real estate agent at Long & Foster and cochairman of the Hispanic Realtor Forum, at the Northern Virginia Association of Realtors.

Perhaps the most chilling evidence of race-based lending patterns came from a study published in 2007 by six big housing advocacy organizations, including the Woodstock Institute and the California Reinvestment Coalition. Entitled "The Cost of the American Dream," the study combed even deeper into the Fed's

data and found racial patterns etched into the organizational structure at Washington Mutual in Seattle, a major player in both prime
and subprime mortgage lending.

WaMu, as most people called Washington Mutual, carefully
segregated its prime and subprime lending into two separate organizations. Low-cost "prime" lending went almost entirely through
Washington Mutual Bank. High-cost subprime loans went almost
entirely through Long Beach Mortgage, one of Orange County's
oldest and most notorious players.

There wasn't anything startling about segregating the middle-
and upper-crust prime borrowers from the sketchier customers
down the food chain. Many of the big banks did the same thing,
especially if they had bought their way into the subprime business.
What was startling, though, was that WaMu's white and nonwhite
customers were ultimately being handled through almost entirely
different organizations.

The Fed data showed that 75.9 percent of WaMu's loans to African-Americans went through Long Beach. By contrast, 80 percent
of WaMu's loans to whites went through Washington Mutual Bank.
The split held up in most parts of the country, but it was particularly
extreme in Charlotte, North Carolina. There, the study reported,
95 percent of WaMu's loans to blacks and 91 percent of its loans to
Hispanics went through Long Beach, the subprime shop.

Sure, it was possible those disparities reflected nothing more
than the different credit risk between whites and nonwhites. But I
wouldn't have put much money on that bet.

———————

As a college-educated white man from a comfortable background, I had always thought about discrimination as a fairly
abstract problem. But that changed in June 2008, when I ran into

two hopping-mad white women who were convinced they had been taken for a ride.

Paula Rush was a single mother in Churchville, Maryland, not far from Baltimore, who had become a latter-day crusader in the mold of Erin Brockovich. Having owned a small business in Florida and two other houses in Maryland, Paula hadn't thought of herself as a financial novice. Indeed, she already had a decent mortgage on her five-bedroom house.

Paula's problems had started in the spring of 2006, when a mortgage broker pitched her a "1 percent" mortgage from American Home Mortgage—my own original lender. Eager to pull some cash out of her house and get a better deal, Paula fell into the same option ARM trap that had snared Miguel and Ana Delgado.

A brown-haired woman with freckly skin, Paula sat down with me at her dining room table and showed me closing documents on her loan. Sure enough, they made it sound like she had gotten the deal of a lifetime. "At present and until further notice your monthly payment is as follows," the American Home's wholesale unit informed her. "Principal and interest: $1,483.00; monthly escrow deposit for taxes: $464.47; monthly escrow payment for insurance: $107.67. . . . Total monthly payment: $2055.14."

On a $586,000 mortgage, that was a delightfully low payment. What Paula had not realized was that the rate would apply for only the first month. Everything seemed fine when she made her first payment in June 2006. But when she got her second billing statement in July, she learned that she had already racked up $3,000 in "deferred interest." Like Ana and Miguel, Paula was stunned and then outraged. She called American Home again and again, but she was stuck. She couldn't get out of the loan, because she had signed hundreds of pages of loan documents. She couldn't refinance, because she had already used some of the extra money she had borrowed.

Instead, Paula went on an investigative rampage. She demanded and eventually got her entire loan file, and she soon found evidence that the broker and the lender had played fast and loose with the facts to get her approved. The appraisal said that her house was a "custom home" and that her basement was finished—neither of which was true, and both of which had helped inflate the home's value. The file also said she had $56,000 in "verified assets," which she had not had. She also found that she had been overcharged by more than $900 on a recordation tax, which was refunded after she confronted American Home.

By September 2006, Paula had sued American Home for fraud and stopped making any payments at all. Her case was still pending when I met her in 2008, and she was still living in her house for free. Meanwhile, though, she had started a cottage business helping other American Home borrowers dig into their own loan files and challenge their loan terms. (I was not one of them, having long since switched to a loan from JPMorgan.)

"We're not disgruntled borrowers—we're victims of a crime," Rush told me. "It was arrogant, it was purposeful, and they did it anyway."

For all her militant intensity, Rush took a somewhat politically incorrect view that women—including her—were more likely to be scammed because they were more trusting than men. "I honestly think women are more trusting, and the brokers know it," she told me. "They didn't try it with you because you're a man, and they're more intimidated by you. But with women, it's different. If you've always dealt with legitimate people, you can't imagine that anyone is going to do something like this to you. You don't see it coming."

At first, I was dubious. She was making the same basic argument made by Ana and Miguel, who had been unsure of themselves and had trusted a mortgage broker who spoke their language. The difference was that Paula was an experienced American who wasn't shy about getting into a fight with bankers. She didn't look gullible to me.

What changed my mind was meeting Laura Beall, a divorced mother and real estate agent in Oakton, Virginia. Laura, who had gone to Paula for help, had also refinanced her house with a mortgage from American Home, just a few months before I got my own loan. By the time I met her in 2008, Laura was suing American Home and had stopped making her payments as well. It turned out that she and I were almost a perfect lab study in the contrast between loans given to two almost identical borrowers by the same lender at about the same time.

Like me, Laura had applied for an interest-only loan from American Home Mortgage in 2004. We both had credit scores that were solidly in the "prime" category, though my score of 720 was slightly higher than hers at 690. On the other hand, Laura had far more equity in her house than I had in mine. Even after extracting cash through the refinancing to help her son buy his own home, Laura had the equivalent of a 25 percent down payment. I was putting only 10 percent down. In other respects, we were indistinguishable: we both had been employed for years by the same company; we earned similar amounts of money; we had long track records as home owners. We even started out with exactly the same interest rate: 5.625 percent.

The differences were in how much we had been forced to pay in up-front fees, and how much our interest rates would go up in the future. And those differences were amazing. I had paid only one "point"—1 percent of the loan amount—as an "origination fee." Laura had had to pay two points. That alone increased Laura's up-front cost by more than $5,000. Next came the interest rate. Under my loan, the interest rate would stay fixed for five years. Under Laura's loan, the rate would start adjusting after only three years.

The killer difference was in how much our respective interest rates would jump once they became adjustable. This figure involved a seemingly innocuous number called the "index margin." When my mortgage went from a fixed rate to an adjustable rate, it would be set at 2.25 percentage points above LIBOR. By contrast, Laura's rate would be 5 percentage points above LIBOR (and two years earlier).

The difference between 2.25 percentage points and 5 percentage points might sound harmless. In actual dollars and cents, though, the difference was lethal. Using one of the many mortgage calculators available on the Internet, I calculated that Laura's monthly payments would have been about $1,000 lower if she had had my index margin rather than hers. "It was a predatory loan," Laura said. "They told me this was the only loan I could qualify for, and I believed them. But obviously, your loan shows that I had other choices and they were taking advantage of me."

I was amazed. As a white man who had grown up in a secure home and gone to a good college, I had been oblivious to this market-based form of discrimination. I knew it existed, and I had seen people spew hatred. Yet, like so many other white-bread men who never felt the sting of second-class treatment, I had been clueless about how much I had benefited from discrimination myself.

With Laura, it seemed irrefutable. There was no other valid explanation. The lenders had stuck her with a more expensive deal because, for some deeply rooted cultural reasons, they knew they could get away with it. Maybe women were more trusting. Maybe they didn't cause as much trouble if they found out they were being cheated.

Whatever the reason, available mortgage data showed that
women were in fact being steered to expensive loans more than
men. A 2006 study by the Consumer Federation of America,
tapping into the same Federal Reserve data as the studies about
racial patterns in mortgage lending, found that women were more
likely than men to end up with subprime mortgages, regardless
of their income level. In fact, the study found that the dispar-
ity between men and women increased as their incomes went up.
Among people who earned more than twice the median income in
their region, women were 50 percent more likely than men to get
a subprime loan.

Laura asked me if she could use my mortgage as evidence in her
lawsuit. Naturally, I was happy to oblige. If I could help her stick it
to the man, it was the least I could do.

13

GOD HELP US ALL

With only a few days left before Christmas 2008, Patty and I were hurtling toward bottom. We had been under so much strain for so long that we were often at each other's throats, jeopardizing the love that had brought us together in the first place. In November, four years after buying the house, we had finally crossed our personal Rubicon and fallen thirty days behind on our mortgage. New Year's day would mark ninety days past due.

"The last thing Chase wants is to foreclose on your home," JPMorgan Chase had written us. It assured us that it wanted to "help" and was willing to evaluate us for a number of "alternatives." If we didn't "resolve" our payment delinquency, it politely warned, "you will lose your home." No surprise there. For months now we could feel our day of reckoning was getting close. What did come as a shock was that the world economy was reaching its own moment of truth at the same time.

Starting in September, thirteen months after the financial crisis had begun, the country had fallen into a self-reinforcing vortex. It was as if on Labor Day somebody had flipped a switch. Almost simultaneously, Wall Street and the "real economy" both went into seizure. Lehman Brothers collapsed over the weekend of September 14 after the Treasury and the Fed refused to rescue it. Merrill Lynch, facing its own likely collapse, cut a deal the same weekend to sell itself to Bank of America, which in turn had to be bailed out by the taxpayers.

By October, the stock market had crashed about 40 percent from its highs earlier in the year. In the waning days of the Bush presidency, the Treasury and the Fed were trying to bail out the entire banking system. The list of zombie corporations included Citigroup, American International Group, Fannie Mae, Freddie Mac, General Motors, Chrysler, and possibly Bank of America.

In hindsight, it became clear that Wall Street's problems had hit the rest of the economy in September, creating the kind of vicious "negative feedback loop" that Fed chief Ben Bernanke had been dreading. Job losses, which had averaged about eighty thousand a month from January through August, accelerated to a jaw-dropping five hundred thousand a month from September through December. Consumers, who had kept on spending even in bad years, were cutting back for the first time in decades. Even the Organization of the Petroleum Exporting Countries (OPEC) was in panic mode as oil prices crashed from $147 a barrel in July to barely $60 a barrel in December.

Everybody, from Middle Eastern investors to bedraggled American shoppers, seemed to have reached the same conclusion at exactly the same time: the United States had suffered a staggering collapse in wealth, and the fallout was about to begin. The most astonishing change was how top policy makers in Washington suddenly jumped through the looking glass, violating almost every principle of traditional economic policy. Policies that were supposed to be bad—trillion-dollar budget deficits, government bailouts, government intrusion in financial markets—were suddenly essential.

On September 18, Treasury Secretary Henry M. Paulson had stunned the world by proposing the biggest taxpayer-financed bailout of business in history. Under Paulson's plan, the government would spend up to $700 billion to buy up "troubled assets"—mostly mortgages and mortgage-backed securities—and get them off the books of banks and other financial institutions.

Bush and Paulson weren't the only ones turning things upside down. The Federal Reserve, that marbled fortress of calm and restraint, went on a money-printing rampage. Between September and the end of December, the Fed had created an extra $1 trillion literally out of nothing. Its official balance sheet ballooned from about $900 billion to $2 trillion in less than four months, and the Fed was frantically pumping that money out through a slew of new lending programs to jump-start the frozen credit markets.

From my vantage point inside the mortgage crisis, I wasn't sure what was more unnerving: my own financial meltdown, and possibly the collapse of my marriage to Patty; or a national meltdown so bad that the president and Federal Reserve were shattering what had seemed like every bedrock principle of our economic system.

———

Patty and I were bracing for our worst Noel. After Christmas, it might be only a matter of weeks before JPMorgan Chase began foreclosure proceedings. Neither of us took any comfort in the fact that we were about to join a record-breaking wave of foreclosures. With delinquency rates still climbing to new records, all the signs pointed toward a staggering 4 million foreclosures in 2009.

We were so tapped out that we could barely buy Christmas presents for the children. I had assumed that one of the fleeting benefits of not paying the mortgage would be that we would have spare cash for other things. Wrong again. Even though Patty had ample work as a freelance book editor, our combined income had been chronically behind our basic living expenses for months. We had a backlog of unpaid bills that would not go away, and we had to postpone gift buying until my next paycheck landed, on Christmas Eve. It was like being a character out of Dickens—Edmund L. Penniless?—except more humiliating.

Not surprisingly, JPMorgan Chase was on our case.

With politicians in Congress screaming about the unwillingness of mortgage lenders to modify loans, Chase had taken out full-page advertisements testifying to the company's eagerness to modify mortgages and keep people in their homes and the availability of alternatives to foreclosure. I had already called Chase in November, in what I could only consider a surreal encounter with those "alternatives."

After getting on the phone with a Chase representative named Sarah and answering her questions about our financial situation, I had learned that I qualified for only a "repayment plan." Instead of getting a break from Chase, I would have to bring my account current by paying an extra $400 a month for six months.

"That wouldn't be much of a help," I had said. "Hasn't Chase been saying it would help borrowers in trouble by modifying loans and reducing the monthly payments?"

"You don't qualify for loan modification," Sarah had replied. "You have to be at least ninety days past due to qualify."

"It sounds as if I would be better off waiting to fall ninety days behind," I had said. "I think I'll wait for that."

Beyond the prospect of losing our house, the real tragedy was what had happened to Patty and me. Four years earlier, we had both been utterly confident that we had each found our soul mate. We had proudly risked everything to be together. It had obviously been a gamble, but it had seemed like a glorious gamble for the kind of love we both had dreamed of for years.

Now our marriage was in tatters. Instead of supporting each other and drawing on each other's strengths, we each blamed the other for our financial nightmare. We lashed out over perceived slights and went around and around in the same arguments, reopening old wounds. I was angry that she wasn't earning close to $40,000 a year, the amount we had originally and naïvely thought she would have to earn. I was even angrier that she had belittled my warnings and accused me of bullying her without ever getting closer to a solution.

Slowly and possibly too late, I realized that I had been a big part of Patty's problems. She looked sadder and more defeated than I had ever imagined possible. Her face was puffy from exhaustion, stress, and crying. Having always been so regal and forceful, she now seemed lost and lonely. "You have chipped away at my soul," she told me. "You chipped away until I had no self-esteem."

Though Patty was racked by guilt at her inability to earn more money, she also bitterly accused me of browbeating her to become someone she had never been. I had courted her relentlessly to come east, and she had uprooted herself and her family to be with me. As soon as she had arrived, I had gone back to my normal workaday life as if nothing had changed, leaving her to flail in utterly unfamiliar surroundings.

"Everything revolves around you," she said. "You get up in the morning, take a shower, and go to work. You work as long as you want and come back when you want, and we're not allowed to question that, because your work is so important. But you have no idea what it's like for me." In her eyes, I had morphed from a gentle and adoring rescuer to a short-tempered, self-absorbed, hypercritical prick.

Amazingly, we still loved each other. I had never known a woman with as much fire and heart as her. I loved nothing more than being with her, whether it was watching television or reading together. As bitter as all the fights were, we always returned to being each other's closest companion.

Patty, for her part, had thrown everything she had into creating a home with me. For all her flaws as a breadwinner, she had succeeded at the much harder task of forming a new family with my boys. She made them feel welcome when they came home after school to hang out with their friends. She cooked meals for them, listened to their sagas about girls, and never turned down friends who wanted to spend the night on weekends. Patty had even managed to endear herself to Matthew, who at first had bluntly predicted that he would always feel like a "guest" in our house. Ryan, who had just started college, confided things to her that he wouldn't tell me.

At the same time, everything had changed for Patty. She had arrived confident, proud, and eager to start a new life. But she had arrived with no money of her own, no job contacts, and only a rough idea of what kind of work she wanted to do. After four years of anxiety, tension, and hurt, she doubted she could go on like this much longer.

Just as I had reverted to my familiar patterns as a reporter, she had reverted to what she knew best: being a homemaker. Yet no matter how much success she had with that, I kept complaining that she wasn't making enough money.

"You have made it impossible for me to find work that is right for me," Patty accused me on more than one occasion, weeping. "I am terrified of you."

You couldn't accuse Henry M. Paulson or Ben S. Bernanke of being afraid to act. Both of them knew immediately that the roof had fallen in on them in September 2008, and both reacted with emergency rescue measures on a scale nobody had ever seen before.

At the Federal Reserve, the spigots were on for a half-dozen lending programs, and it began buying up mortgage-backed securities in a bid to push down rates on home loans. The volume of bank reserves shot up more from September through December than it had during the Fed's entire ninety-five-year history since 1913.

Paulson, at the Treasury, proposed his eye-popping $700 billion plan to rescue the financial industry. For sheer bravado, it was hard to beat Paulson's three-page explanation of how the Treasury would spend that money (short version: any way it wanted). For all the money getting thrown around, there was an air of unreality when Paulson described what he thought was causing the crisis and what he would fix.

To hear Paulson tell it, the crisis had very little to do with the fact that the United States had just lost about $12 trillion in wealth as a result of the combined collapses in housing prices and stock prices. Nor did it have much to do with the fact that about 4 million home owners might lose their homes in 2009. Nor did it reflect a fundamental illness in the financial system. The way he saw it, the root of the crisis was more like a technical glitch: banks were stuck with hundreds of billions of dollars' worth of mortgage-backed securities that didn't have a value, because no one wanted to buy them.

"These illiquid assets are clogging up our financial system, and undermining the strength of our otherwise sound financial institutions," he declared on September 19, the day after he had first presented his idea for a rescue plan to House and Senate leaders. The reference to "otherwise sound financial institutions" was telling. Paulson did not think that most banks were sick. It was just their assets that were sick, for now at least. Paulson confidently asserted that the government would eventually get much if not all of the bailout money back.

Neither Treasury nor Fed officials ever took a stab at explaining whether there were any real losses, and how big those losses might be. It was a crucial question, and they were ignoring it. On the basis of just the fall in housing prices since 2006, economists were estimating that the United States had lost about $6 trillion in housing wealth.

Some of that wealth had come and gone without ever being missed, but an enormous share of those losses was utterly real. Almost half of all the $600 billion worth of subprime mortgages made in 2006 were delinquent, and at least one-quarter of them were likely to end up in foreclosure.

Right from the start, a number of hard-boiled and quite conservative economists protested that the economy's real problem wasn't the financial institutions with their "clogged pipelines." It was that the housing market had abruptly eliminated trillions of dollars of wealth. "Why aren't they addressing the real problem, which is the collapse of the housing market?" asked Christopher Mayer, vice dean at Columbia University's business school and a veteran analyst of the housing and mortgage markets.

"If we're going to pour $700 billion into the same financial companies that helped cause this crisis in the first place, I think we should at least take some of that money and put it straight into subsidizing cheap mortgages." Mayer, who considered himself a Republican, argued that pouring money into cheap mortgages would help existing home owners by making it easier to sell or refinance their homes. It would also boost home prices, which would boost the value of all those toxic mortgage-backed securities that were clogging up the pipelines.

Mayer wasn't the only one with ideas like that. Glenn Hubbard, dean of the Columbia Business School and a top economic adviser to President George W. Bush in his first term, teamed up with Mayer to craft a more detailed proposal. Martin Feldstein, professor of economics at Harvard University and top adviser to President Reagan, developed proposals of his own.

In Congress, Democrats were screaming at Paulson to do something to help distressed borrowers. Liberals wanted to help people in trouble. Conservatives wanted to put money where it would have the biggest economic impact. Both camps were ending up at the same place: home owners. Paulson wanted none of that. Congress had specifically instructed the Treasury to use some of its money to reduce mortgage foreclosures, and yet he never took any meaningful action on that front.

The Treasury and the Fed also both bent over backward to avoid taking any semblance of control of the banks and financial institutions that they were plowing money into. There was a clear Republican worldview behind this. The way Paulson saw it, taking control of failed banks was a strategy for European countries with their market socialism and their social contracts. In shoring up healthy institutions, by contrast, the United States wouldn't be bailing out failures and thus didn't need to take control over them. Instead, the government would be "investing" in solid institutions.

It quickly became clear in the case of Citigroup that distinguishing between "bailing out" a sick institution and "investing" in a healthy institution with sick assets was going to prove difficult. In November 2008, the Treasury and the Fed were forced to inject a second round of capital into Citigroup, the nation's biggest bank-holding company. Citigroup, which was undeniably on the unofficial list of banks that were "too big to fail," was racking up massive new losses tied both to its remaining portfolio of toxic mortgage-backed securities and to mounting loan defaults on all kinds of loans tied to the deepening recession.

By almost any realistic calculation of its assets and liabilities, Citigroup was a failing institution. Investors had slashed the price of its shares from $54 in May 2007 to about $8 at the time of its second infusion of federal cash in November 2008. It was mathematically impossible for the company to raise enough fresh capital without giving the new investors a controlling stake.

Yet once again, the Treasury and the Fed engaged in extraordinary gymnastics to deny themselves control of the bank. The Treasury "invested" $20 billion in exchange for preferred shares and agreed to insure Citigroup against potential losses on $300 billion worth of its toxic assets. In theory, the Treasury and the Fed were not so much "investing" in Citigroup as they were selling insurance. In practice, it was a sham.

Citigroup had been one of the worst contributors to the mortgage fiasco, as both a subprime lender and a prolific producer of mortgage-backed securities. Now the company was all but broke, and it was so big that its collapse really could pose a threat to the whole financial system. At this point, the system was so sick that anything could topple it.

Yet the Treasury had now provided Citigroup with two infusions of capital, totaling $45 billion, and it had put taxpayers at risk for billions of dollars in additional losses through the insurance it was providing. In fact, the federal government would be on the hook if Citigroup's toxic portfolios lost more than 10 percent of their value. With everything else collapsing, that seemed like a real possibility.

All of this added up to very bad news for Barack Obama as he prepared to move into the White House on January 20, 2009. The steepening recession during the fall had made everything worse, clobbering the financial system with new losses as unemployment climbed. By the end of 2008, the country had lost 2.6 million jobs and the bottom was nowhere in sight. As Obama and his top economic advisers made their preparations, they were already getting reports that the nation's banks would need a lot more than $700 billion.

The reckoning had begun.

Dean Baker, codirector of the Center for Economic and Policy Research, estimated that falling home prices had wiped out $6 trillion in wealth since the bubble's peak in 2006, though prices were still falling. Baker's estimate was fairly simple: At the bubble's peak in 2006, the Federal Reserve had estimated the total value of housing, at about $21.8 trillion. The best measure of home prices, the Case-Shiller index of prices in twenty major metropolitan areas, had dropped more than 25 percent since then.

On top of the $6 trillion in lost housing wealth, Baker noted, stock prices had fallen almost 40 percent from their high point in July. That drop translated to an additional $6 trillion hit to our collective balance sheet.

Even in an economy as enormous as that of the United States, $12 trillion was a staggering amount to lose. In effect, it was almost as much as the nation's 2008 gross domestic product: $14.4 trillion. Even if a lot of that wealth had been a figment of the imagination, investors and lenders had been making decisions on the assumption that it was real. Losing the equivalent of almost a full year of economic activity had to have consequences.

On the basis of empirical research, economists have estimated for years that the "wealth effect" from home prices—the amount people raise or lower their spending in response to each dollar up or down in the value of their house—is about 6 percent. If the value of your house climbs by $10,000, you are likely to increase your spending by about $600. Because stock prices are much more volatile, people seem to change their spending by only three cents for every $1 shift in their investment portfolio.

Those numbers are very rough, and people's behavior can be affected by all kinds of special circumstances. The special circumstance for the US economy now is that most Americans have not been saving enough for retirement. That's true in part because people had been counting on their homes as their most important source of retirement "saving."

Christmas Eve was looking to be a nightmare.

We had been totally broke since Monday, unable to buy presents for the children or even a Christmas tree until my paycheck landed on Wednesday. Making matters worse, Patty had barely spoken to me since Monday.

Our fight had been a familiar one, triggered by money. Patty and I had been drinking coffee in the living room when we discovered that our Internet service had stopped. The Verizon representative told Patty that we owed about $300, and that it would not restore service until we had paid the bill. With just over $400 in our bank account, we would be lucky if we could pay the bill and still keep enough food on the table until Wednesday, Christmas Eve.

"I just wish," I had said miserably, "that you could have done something two years ago that would have helped us avoid this."

I might as well have told her that Argentines were the most obnoxious people I had ever met, and they weren't any good at soccer either. "You son of a bitch," she had snapped. "You just can't stop yourself from sticking the knife in, can you? You just look for every opportunity to go on the attack. Admit it! You wish you'd never married me. You think this was a huge mistake."

Patty always vented her rage before her grief. In situations like this, she wouldn't dream of letting me see her vulnerable. She had marched off to a different room, refusing to speak to me.

Now, three days later, Patty still wasn't speaking to me, except for functional purposes. Emily and I went to buy a Christmas tree, brought it back, and set it up in the living room. Within a few minutes, Patty appeared in the living room, putting on her coat. "I'm going out to do shopping," she announced curtly. "Remember," she added, looking at me, "we agreed that you and I were not going to get each other any gifts. I'm just buying for Emily and the boys."

I hated being cut off from Patty. I hated the conflict, but I also hated sinking ever deeper into financial oblivion. I worked too hard to feel this broke. What had happened to us?

Money had become the taboo topic in our home, impossible to discuss in any way or on any level. It didn't seem to matter where the conversation started. Patty was too skewered by guilt, and I was too worn out from the stress. At some point quite soon, we would have to deal with the question of whether we could really live in our house. I had my doubts.

Yet for all the anger and hurt and insanity, Patty was still The One. She had been so inexplicable, baffling, and contrary that she had forced me to imagine her thoughts and feelings in ways I had never tried before. I hadn't succeeded, but I could now imagine that it was actually possible to look at life in a completely different way than I did. The more I struggled to imagine life from Patty's side, the more intrigued I became.

Slowly, ever so slowly, I realized I had been foolish to think she could just jump into an alien cubicle culture. I really had been a self-absorbed, short-tempered prick. I had fallen in love with the mesmerizing, entrancing, fashionable, and loving part of Patty. She had delivered on all that and more. But I had assumed that the money-earning part of her would come for free.

Amazingly, I didn't regret buying the house. As a financial matter, it had been an unmitigated disaster. On an emotional level, it had in some ways paid off. It had rescued our children from the trauma and turmoil of our divorces and remarriage. It had been a character in their lives, almost like a watchful nanny. Even though Patty and I were unsure if we could endure another day together, our children were all thriving. Ryan had already finished his first year of college. Daniel and Matthew, now seniors, had been accepted to college. They played together in a rock band, and they were enjoying high school the way it was meant to be enjoyed.

The house had allowed my boys to transfer to the schools in our neighborhood, and it had helped them make friends who had stayed close all through high school. Neither the boys nor Emily cared how dilapidated our furniture was. To Emily, we seemed to be near the center of everything. She had an enduring if tempestuous friendship with Oliver, the freckle-faced son of our friends Liz and Dave who lived around the corner. She had Daschel, our loopy golden retriever.

I looked at the clock—3:30 p.m. Even though Patty and I had agreed not to buy each other presents, I suddenly felt a compulsion to get out anyway. Daniel, who was driving my ex-wife's car, agreed to give me a lift to the shopping mall. I would have to take a bus back. With $60 in my wallet, I set out randomly to find a few things that would make Patty smile. I was enjoying myself for what seemed to be the first time in months.

I skipped past all the usual last-minute gifts—gloves, perfume, scarves, jewelry. As I walked past Radio Shack, I remembered that Patty had been moaning for weeks that the wireless mouse for her computer was broken. I found one for $25. Then I saw simple corded telephones on sale for just $10, and remembered her mentioning that we needed one for our bedroom. I bought that. Knowing that Patty had a soft spot for candy, I wandered into a gourmet candy shop and carefully selected a half pound of jelly beans for $5. For a twist, I scooped a quarter pound of shiny, gold-wrapped chocolate coins into a bag as well.

When I got back, Patty was busy making a Christmas dinner for us and all the kids. As angry as she might be with me, she never seemed to stop caring for our children.

"Where have you been?" she asked, puzzled.

"Um, out shopping. I realized I hadn't gotten anything for you."

"Why did you do that?" she asked, sounding irritated. "You know we agreed not to buy gifts for each other. I haven't bought anything for you."

"I know," I said. "I just got the urge to get you a couple little things. It was fun."

Her face softened as she looked at me.

"You know this doesn't affect whether we break up or not?"

"I know, I know. But hey, let's take it one day at a time. Merry Christmas, Patty. How about a hug and a kiss?"

She softened a bit more, and then she smiled and opened her arms.

"Merry Christmas," she said.

We didn't know whether we would be thrown out of our house, whether JPMorgan Chase would cut an unexpectedly generous deal with us, or whether the US government would come riding to the rescue. President Obama announced a $75 billion program aimed at helping about 4 million homeowners avoid foreclosure, though it was unclear whether the program would help us.

Regardless of what happened to the house, I decided to make a rough calculation of how much Patty and I had damaged our personal net worth during our saga with the housing bust. After all, we were both fifty-three and reaching the point where we had to start thinking about retirement. And by any reckoning, we were much less prepared than we had been back in 2004. Not that I had been well prepared to begin with. After the roughly fifty-fifty split with my ex-wife, I had been left with about $100,000 in stock, another $102,000 in my 401(k) retirement account, and the bulk of my defined-benefit pension plan from the *Times*.

That wouldn't have been nearly enough to retire at anything like my old income. But how much had I been set back from there?

At first glance, we had not actually lost so much money on the house itself. We had bought it for $460,000 in August 2004. Although prices had seemed inflated even then, the sale prices in our neighborhood had actually jumped almost 20 percent higher before the market peaked in mid-2006. Since then, according to estimates by Zillow.com and other sources, prices had fallen back to exactly the same level as when we bought in August 2004. That didn't sound too bad.

Unfortunately, that was not the whole story. For starters, there was the question of transaction costs. Between the closing costs we had paid to buy the house and the real estate commissions we would probably have to pay to sell it, we were likely to lose about $35,000 if we sold the house for our original purchase price.

On top of that, when we refinanced in 2006 we had pulled an extra $65,000 out of the house to pay off debts, using up our original 10 percent down payment and increasing our mortgage debt to $479,000. If we were lucky enough to sell the house for what we had originally paid, we would still be "underwater" to the tune of $19,000. That brought the losses up to $54,000.

Hmm. That wasn't good, but it wasn't a horrible calamity. Maybe the wider housing collapse wasn't such a catastrophe either.

Alas, no. As Dean Baker noted, stock prices had collapsed almost 40 percent from their high point in 2008. Unfortunately, virtually all my 401(k) money was invested in stocks. And although it had climbed from $102,000 in 2004 to $145,000 at the end of 2007, it had plunged to just $88,681 by January 2009.

At this point I was beginning to get queasy. My net worth was down about $68,000. It would take years to replace that much money, even if I saved as much as I possibly could. Then there was one more loss, arguably the biggest one of all: four years of lost savings.

Until my divorce, I had been able to set aside about 10 percent of my income for retirement. These days, that would be about $12,000 a year, which would jump to $15,000 after the *Times* made its matching contribution. If Patty and I had lived in a modest apartment, I might have been able to resume those savings. Even if I had parked all the money in an ultraconservative money market fund, I would have still accumulated more than $60,000.

The bottom line: if we had never bought our house, I would have been about $128,000 wealthier than I was now. Not only that, but I would have realized that wealth without taking any investment risks, killing my credit rating, or destroying my marriage. And maybe if I had gotten lucky, I wouldn't have a nagging credit card bill of about $9,000.

There was a larger significance to all this: I would probably not be consuming in the grand American style for many years to come. If we somehow returned to decent saving habits and put away at least 10 percent of our incomes, it would take about ten years just to get back to the starting line on savings.

While our misadventure had certainly been more extreme than those of many other Americans, our situation was not all that unusual. Millions of people had stopped saving over the previous five years, many because they assumed that the rising value of their homes would constitute their main nest egg at retirement. Now we all would have to reexamine that assumption and figure out how to make up for lost time.

Unlike the average American, I was lucky enough to still have a defined-benefit pension plan. If *The New York Times* made good on its obligations, that plan entitled me to about one-third of my income at retirement for the rest of my life. It wasn't enough in itself, but it was a start.

Most Americans, even if they had been saving more than I had, were not so lucky. Back in the early 1980s, about 82 percent of all workers in the United States took part in an old-fashioned defined-benefit program that would guarantee at least some income as long as they lived. Today, barely one-third of workers have a defined-benefit plan. A study compiled by the Center for Retirement

Research at Boston College showed that most Americans are not saving through 401(k) plans anywhere near what they will need for retirement. In 2004, according to the center, the average American between the age of fifty-five and sixty-four had accumulated only $60,000 in his or her retirement account.

President Obama, who inherited the biggest economic catastrophe of any president since Franklin Delano Roosevelt, summed up the country's plight well in his speech to Congress one month after he took office in January 2009: "We have lived through an era where too often, short-term gains were prized over long-term prosperity," he said. "A surplus became an excuse to transfer wealth to the wealthy instead of an opportunity to invest in our future. Regulations were gutted for the sake of a quick profit at the expense of a healthy market. People bought homes they knew they couldn't afford from banks and lenders who pushed those bad loans anyway. And all the while, critical debates and difficult decisions were put off for some other time on some other day."

"Well," he continued, "that day of reckoning has arrived, and the time to take charge of our future is here."

Acknowledgments

This book would not have been possible without enormous support from many different quarters. Had it not been my great luck to work at *The New York Times*, I might never have had the opportunity to see this epic crisis unfold at close range—from Washington and Wall Street to the epicenter of subprime lending in southern California. Despite their enormous misgivings, my editors agreed to let me take time off in the midst of the meltdown to work on this book. I owe a huge debt to all of them, but especially to Dean Baquet and Paula Dwyer in Washington and to Lawrence Ingrassia, Jill Abramson, and Bill Keller in New York. I thoroughly expect them to extract repayment in the quintessentially merciless way that the *Times* has refined to perfection. But they are entitled.

I would also like to thank Robert D. Reischauer, president of the Urban Institute, who provided me with an office and helped me tap into some of the country's brightest minds on economic policy and housing. The Urban Institute is a beacon of public-spirited, nonpartisan, and innovative thinking. It was refreshing just to breathe its air.

As the book neared completion, far behind schedule, Brendan Curry at W. W. Norton managed to thoroughly and thoughtfully edit the manuscript under excruciating time pressure. I am deeply grateful.

I would also like to recognize a handful of organizations that provided some of the earliest, shrewdest, and most thoughtful warnings about the mess we were getting into. The Center for Responsible Lending—a nonprofit advocacy group for borrowers and home owners—brilliantly showed that the subprime mortgages would lead to a tsunami of foreclosures. Dean Baker, codirector of the Center for Economic and Policy Research, relentlessly warned as early as 2003 that a housing bubble had formed and that it would end in tears. And several dedicated community groups—the National Community Reinvestment Coalition, the California Reinvestment Coalition, the Greenlining Institute—richly documented how abusive lenders were targeting the most vulnerable people in our society. As a middle-class, middle-aged white man who always considered himself a reflexive free-market capitalist, I learned that left-of-center critics often understand the business better than the smart-money people do.

Last but not least, I would like to acknowledge the contributions of the late Edward M. Gramlich—Ned, to his legions of friends and admirers. As an economist and longtime Fed governor, Ned devoted much of his life to studying poverty and housing. He saw both the virtues and dangers of innovations in mortgage lending, and he was a voice of unparalleled wisdom and reason on the subject. At least as important, he was a selfless and gentle human being who threw himself into public policy for one simple reason: he cared. No one who knew him will forget him.